Paintings
Of
David
James
Pascoe

David J. Pascoe

a zenosox art book

Paintings of David James Pascoe--copyright ©2020 by zenosox books. All Rights Reserved.

All rights Reserved. No part of this book may be reproduced in any form or by any electronic or mechanical means, including information storage and retrieval systems, without permission in writing from the author. The only exception is by a reviewer, who may quote short excerpts in a review.

Cover designed by David J. Pascoe

David J. Pascoe, author

David J. Pascoe, editor

David J. Pascoe, photographer

Visit my website at www.zenosox.com

Printed in the United States of America

First Printing

Dec 2020

Paperback ISBN:-979-8-5863-2367-5

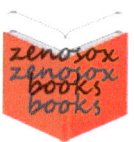

Made WITH Affinity Publisher

PAINTINGS

Late 70s-early 80s

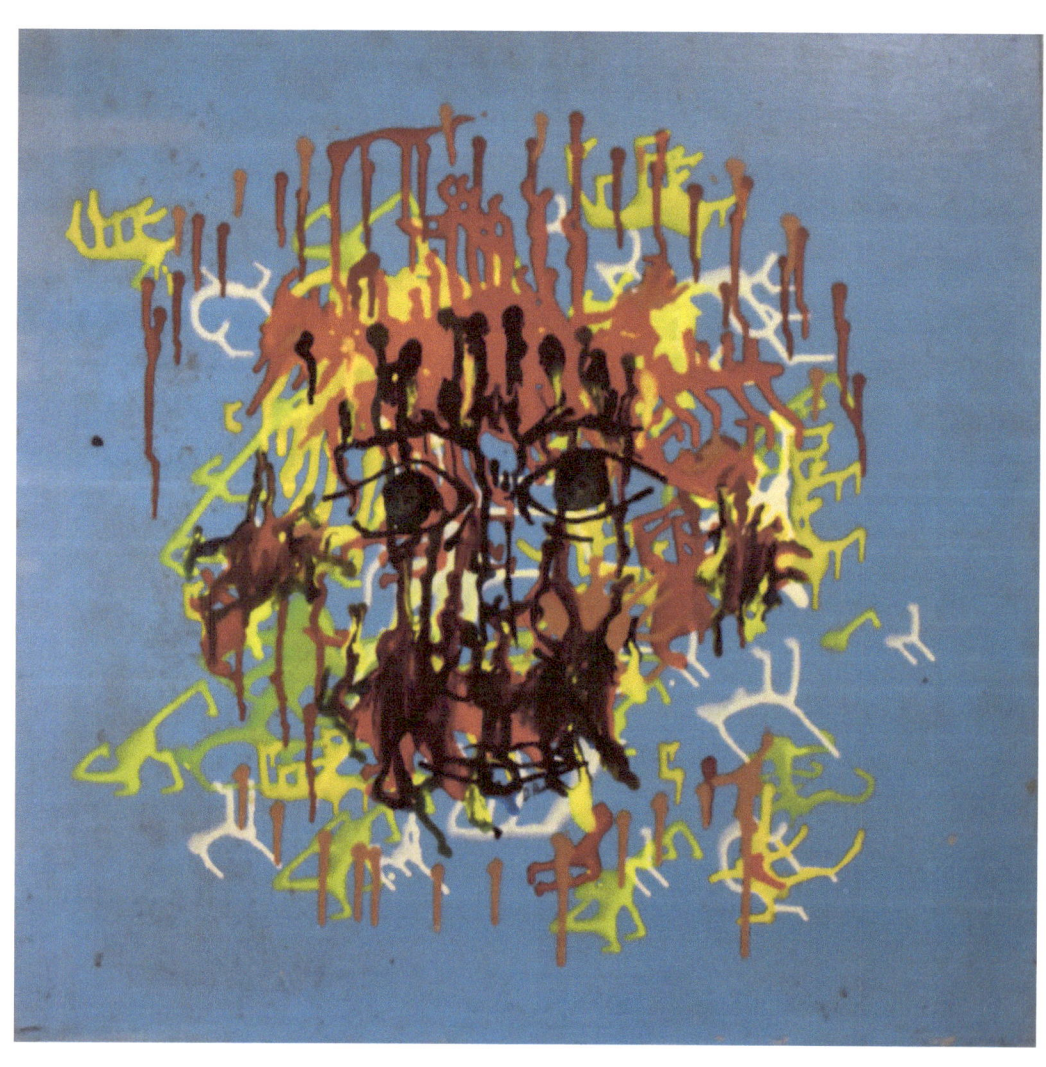

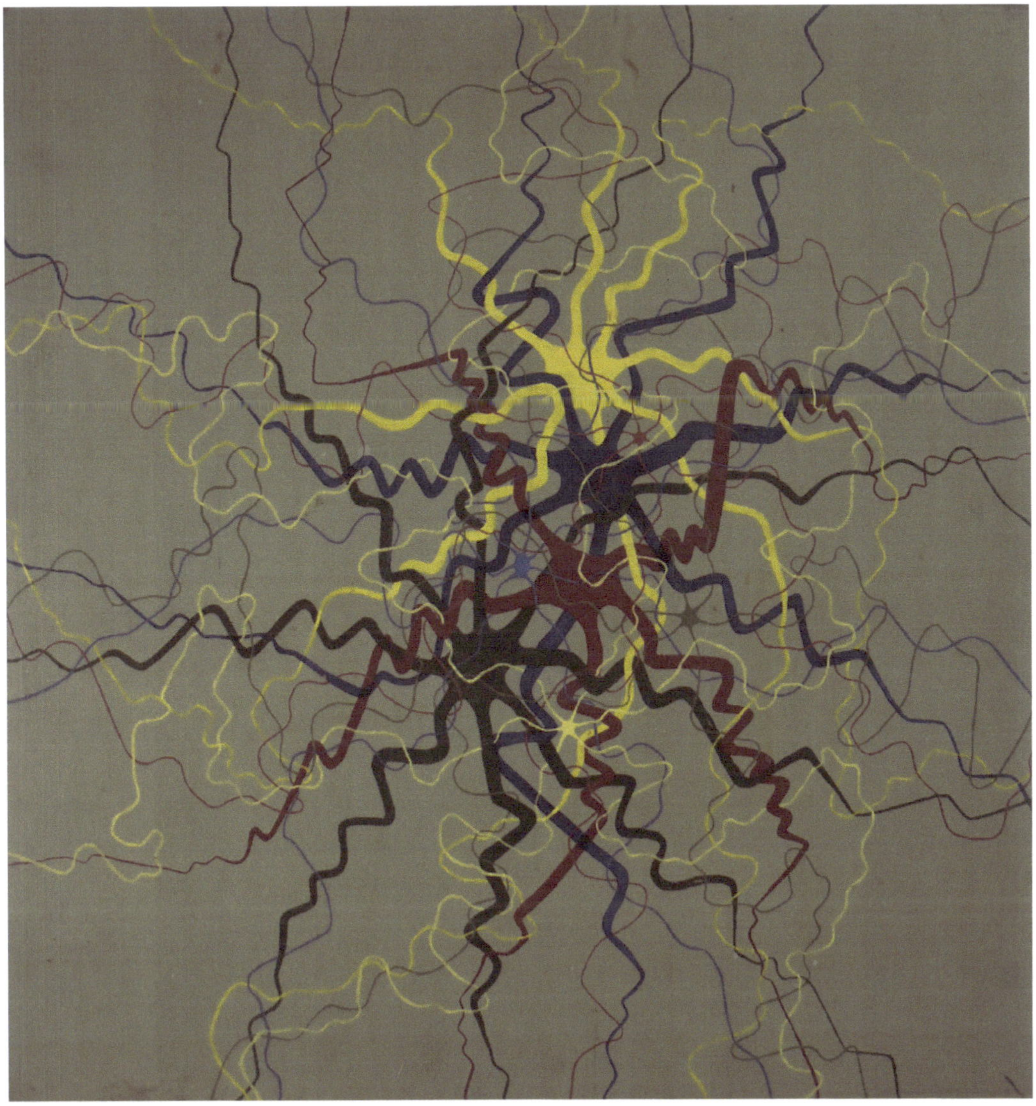

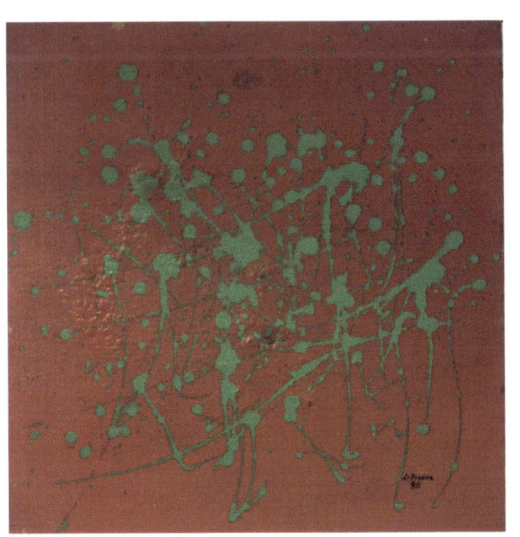
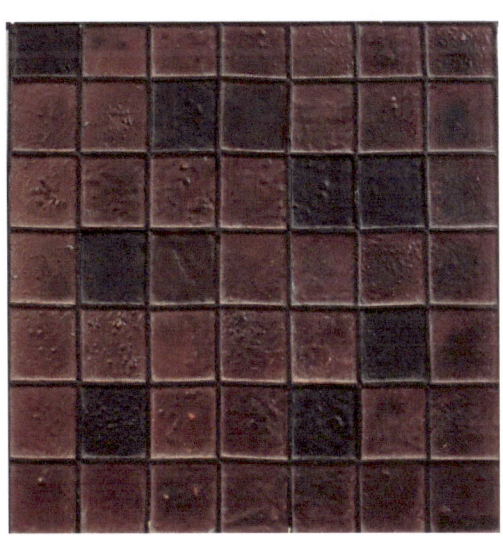

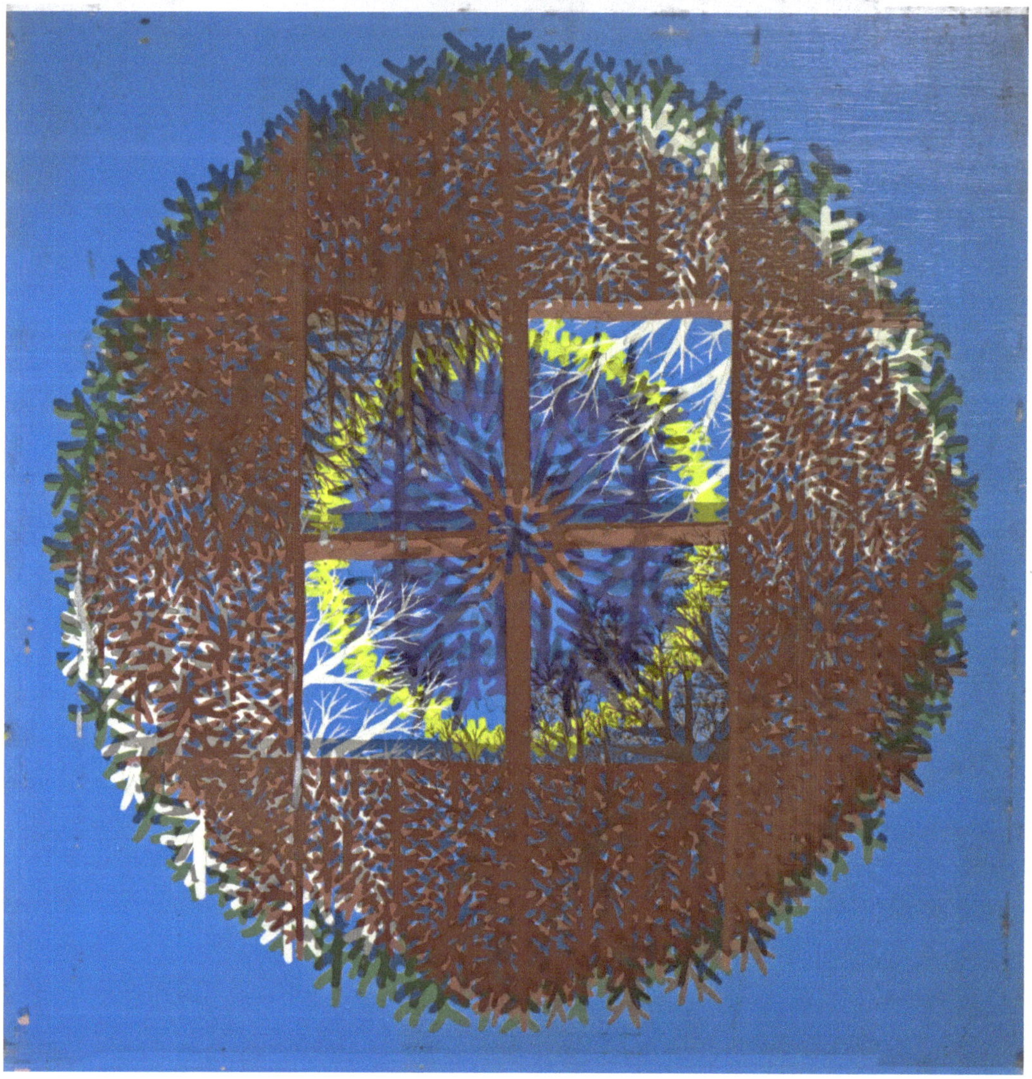

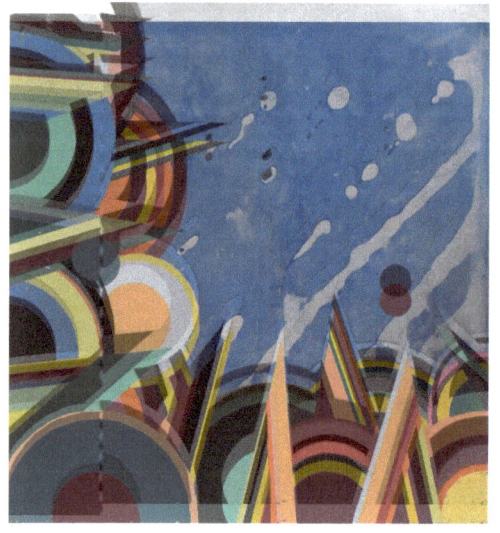
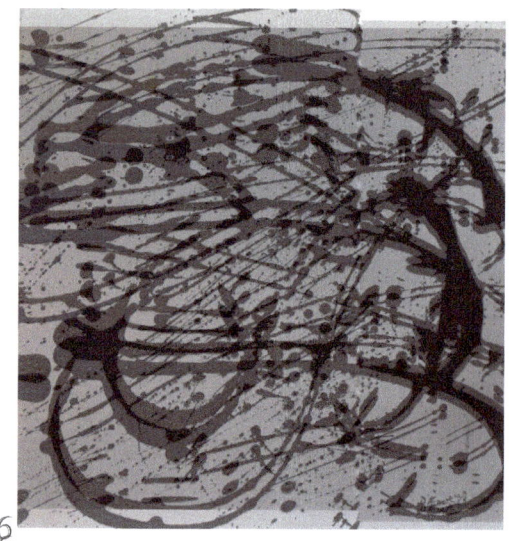

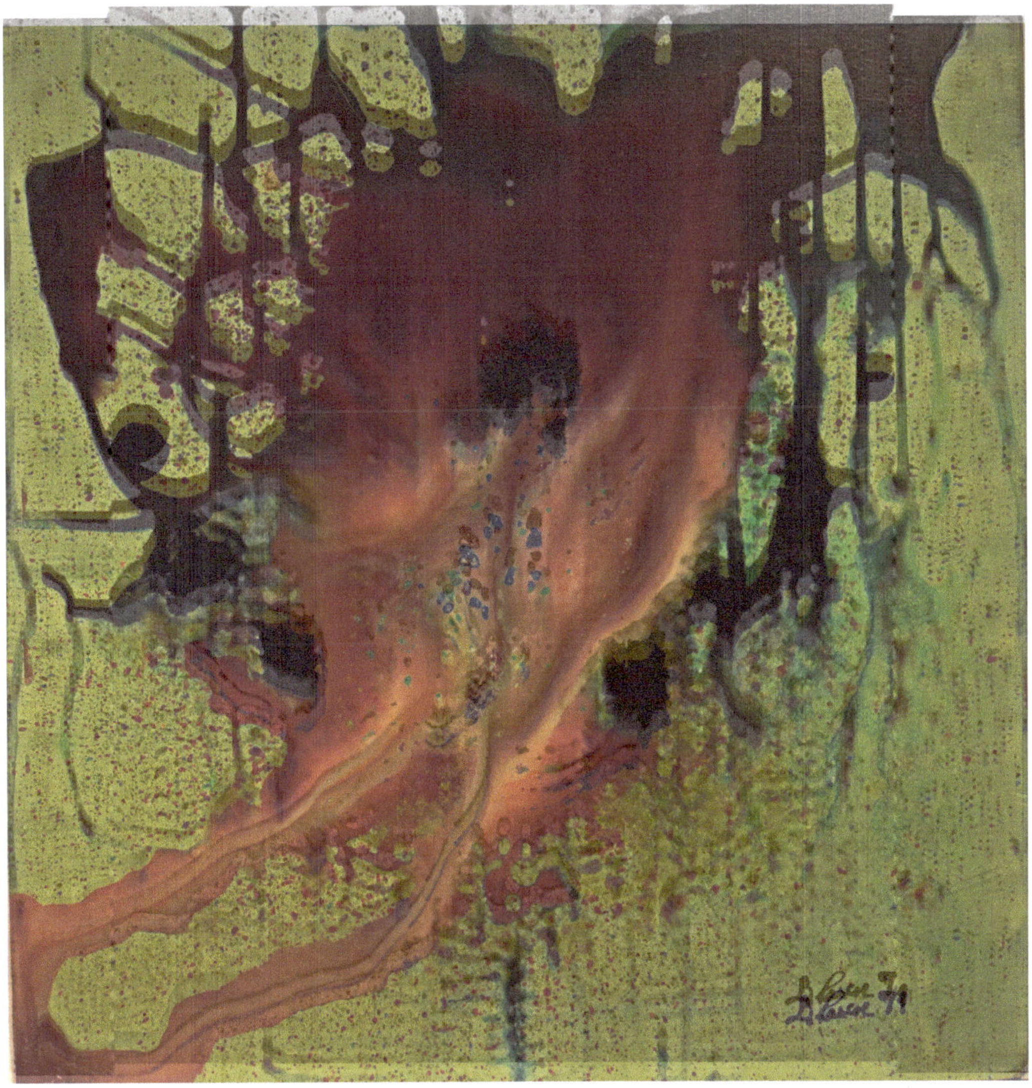

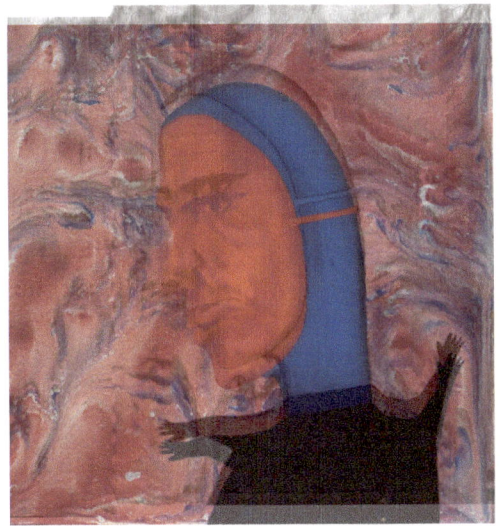
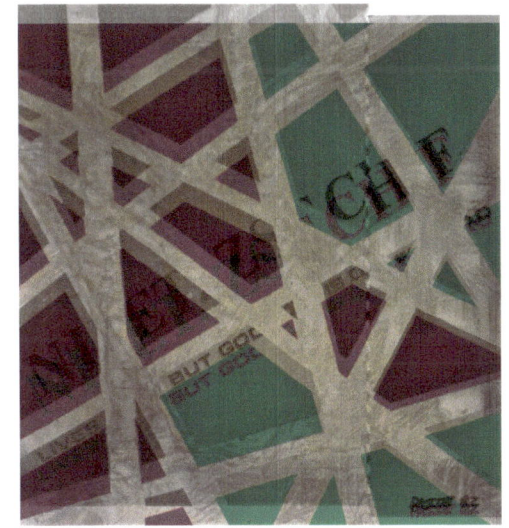

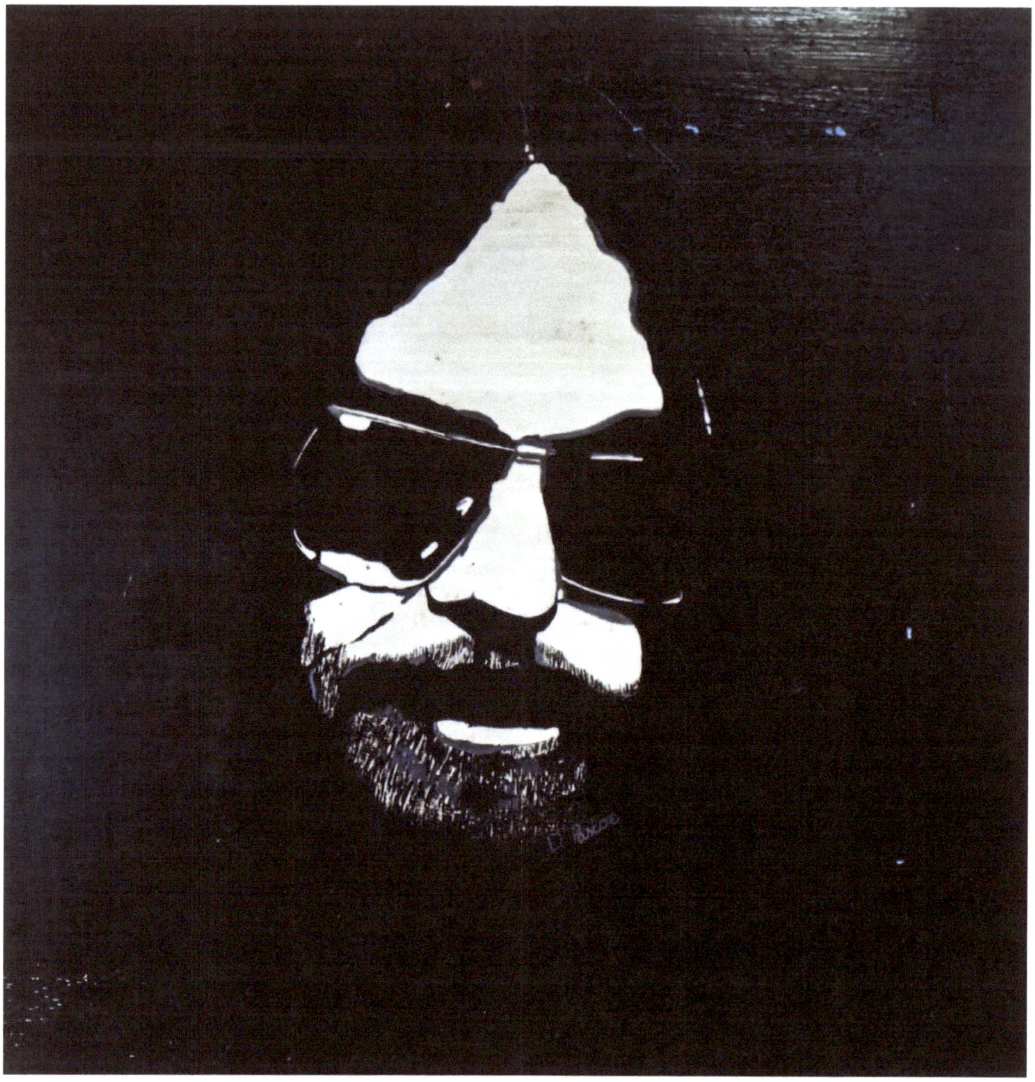

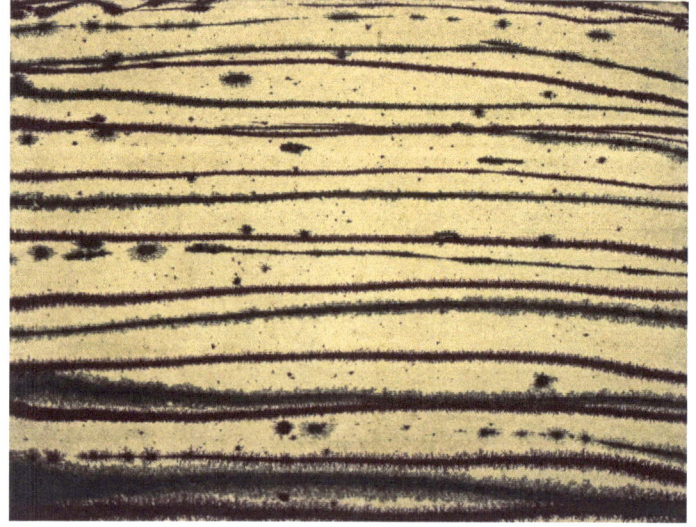

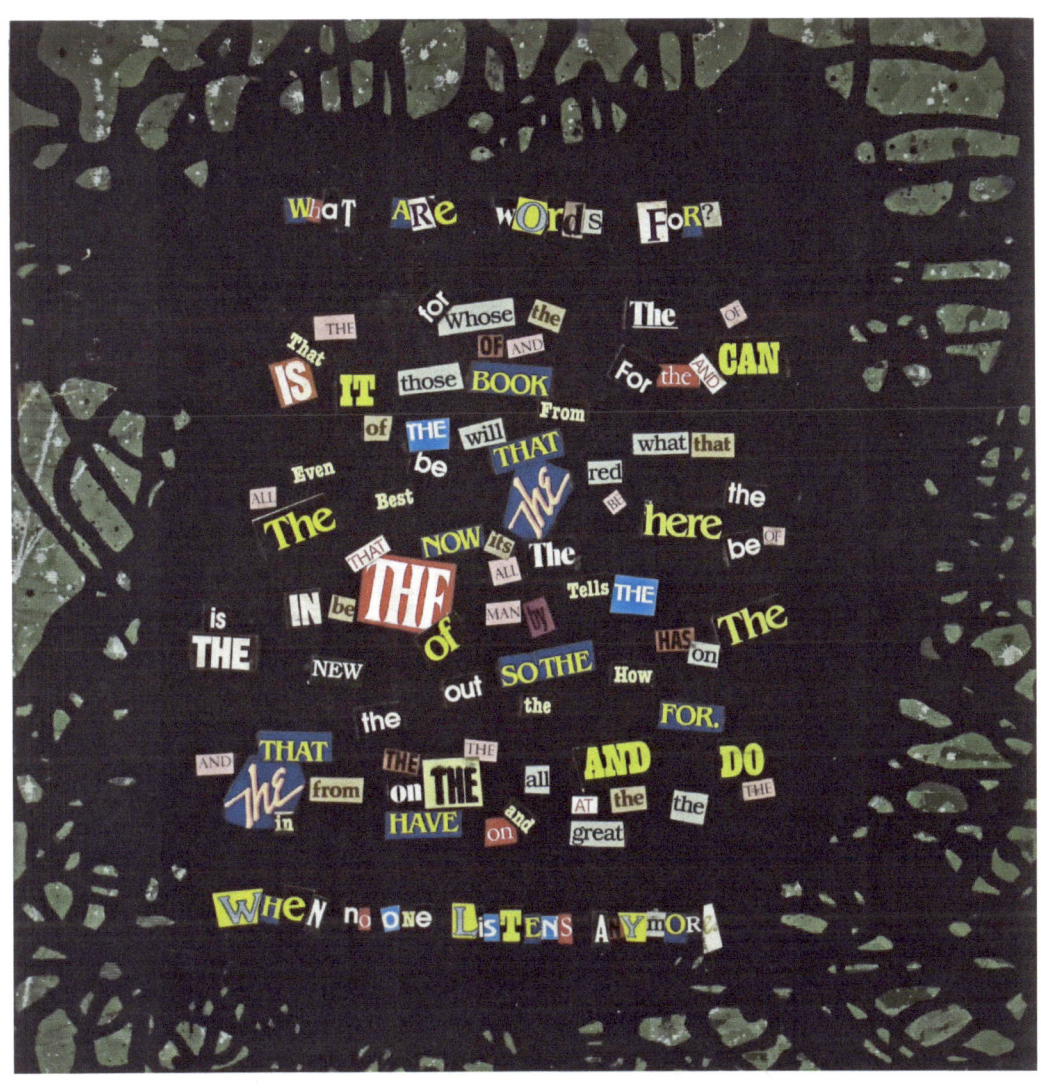

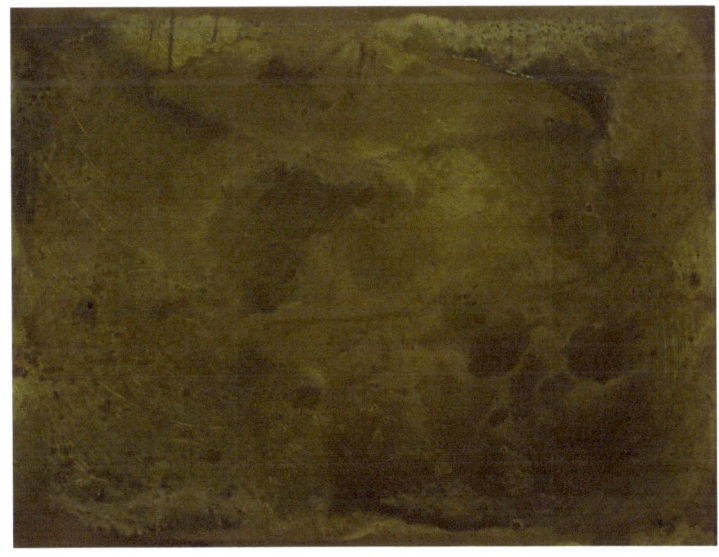

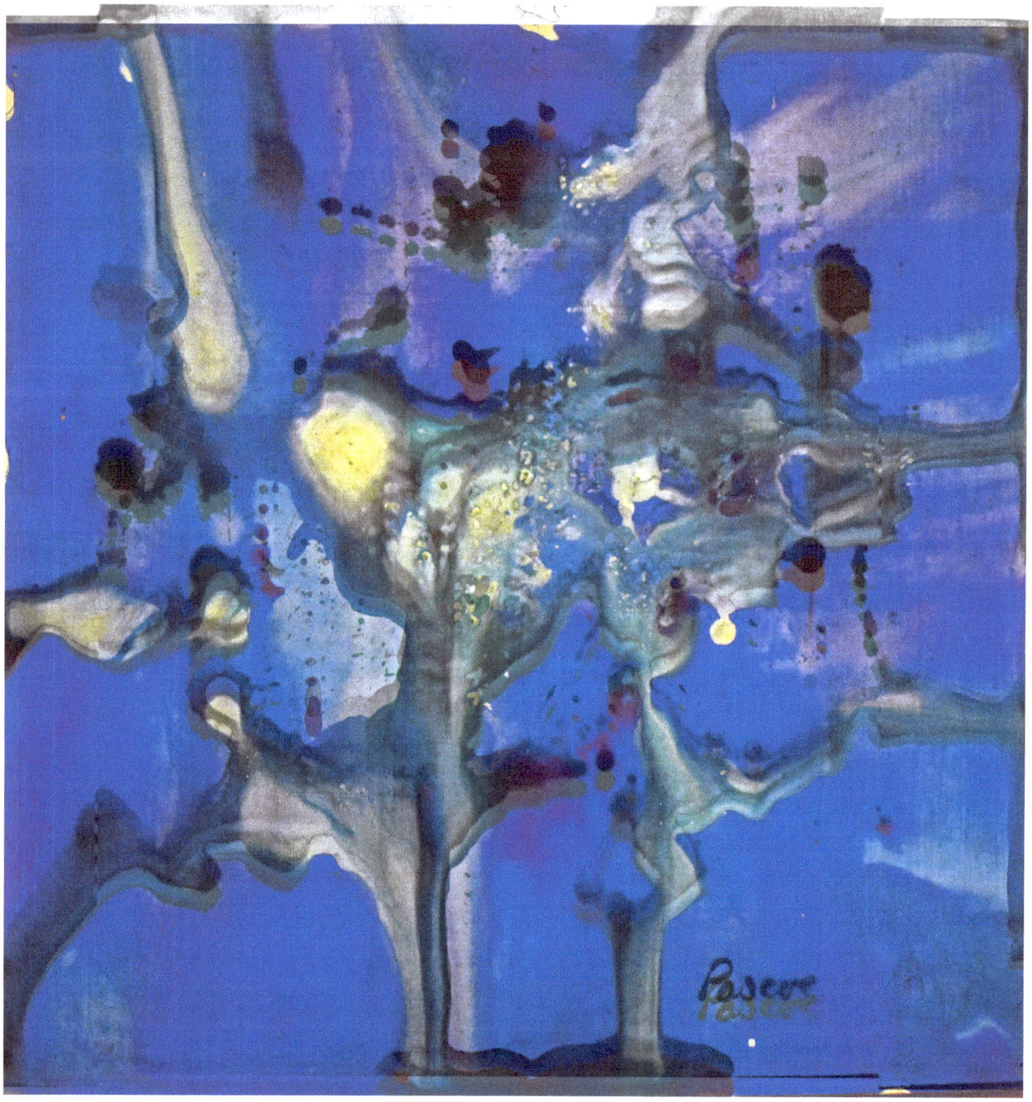

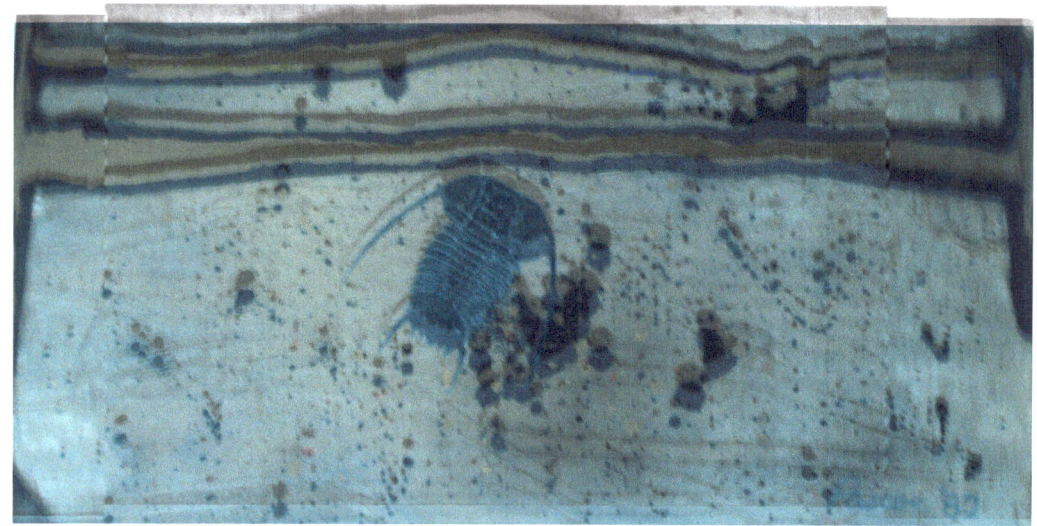

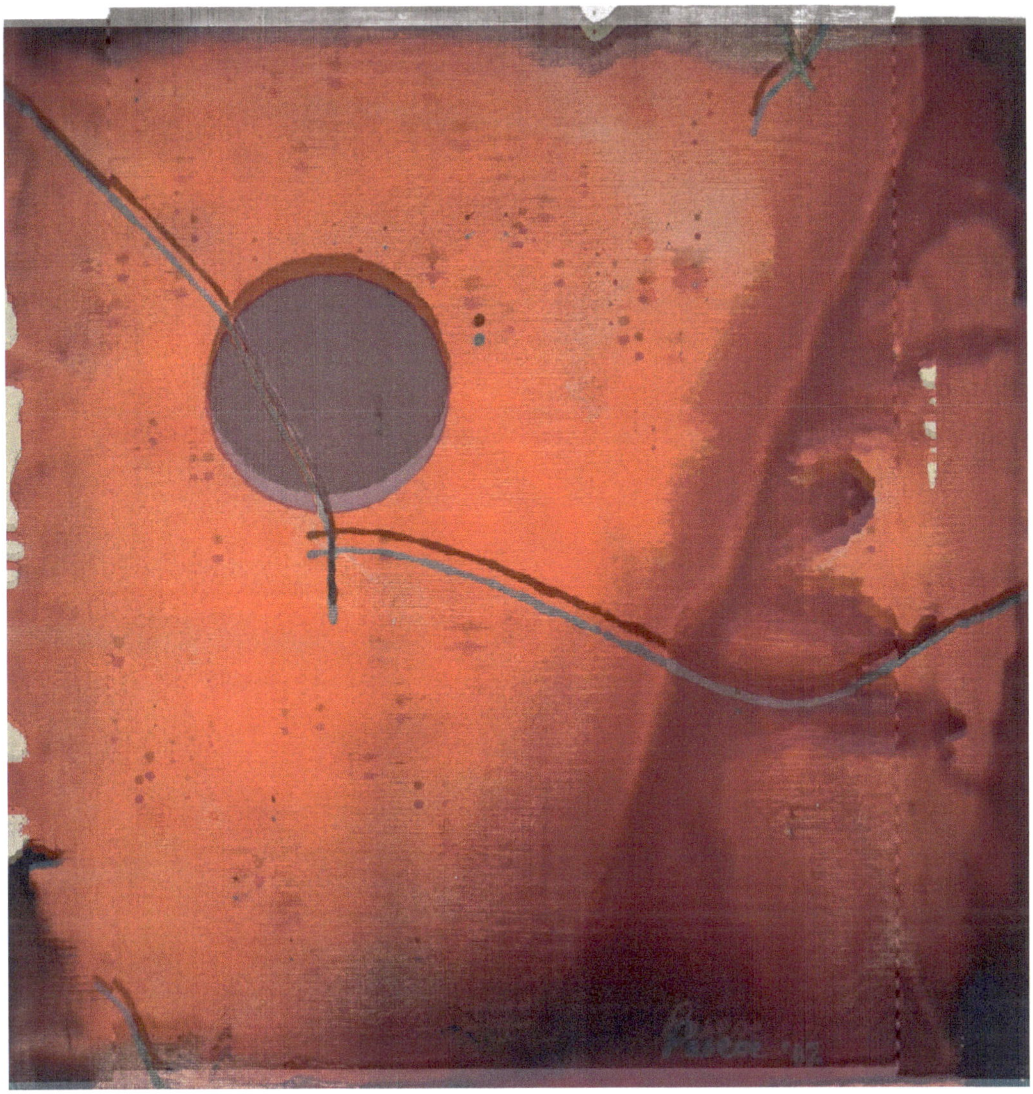

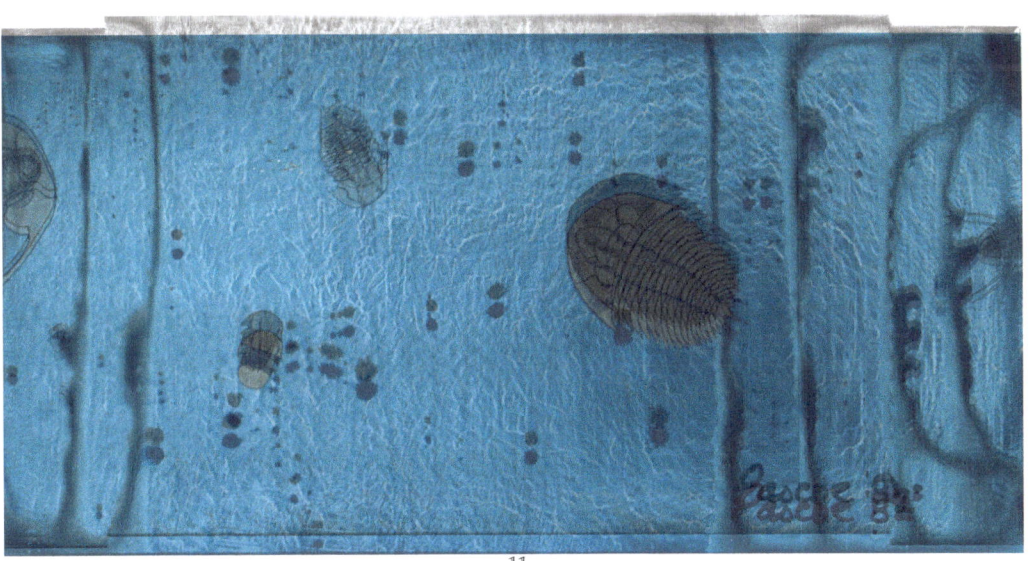

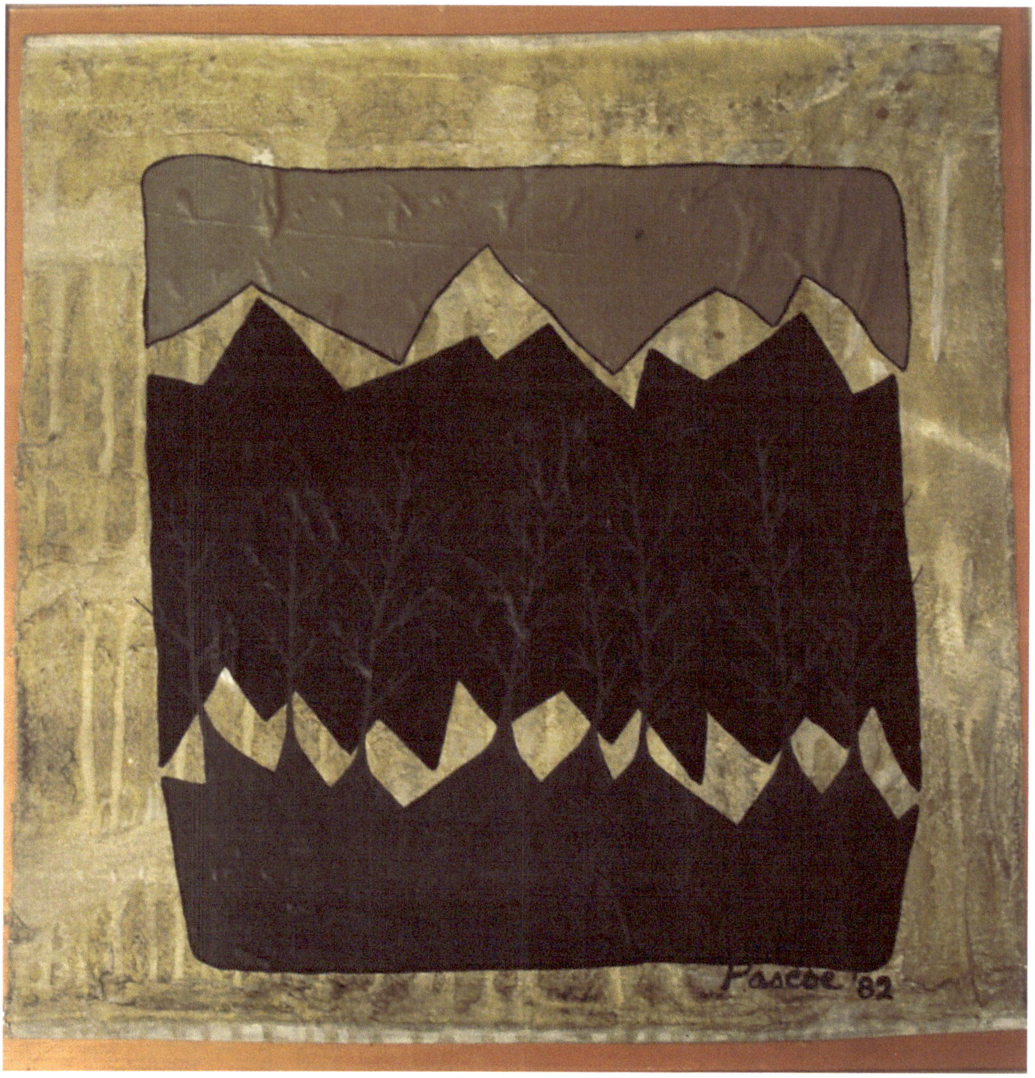

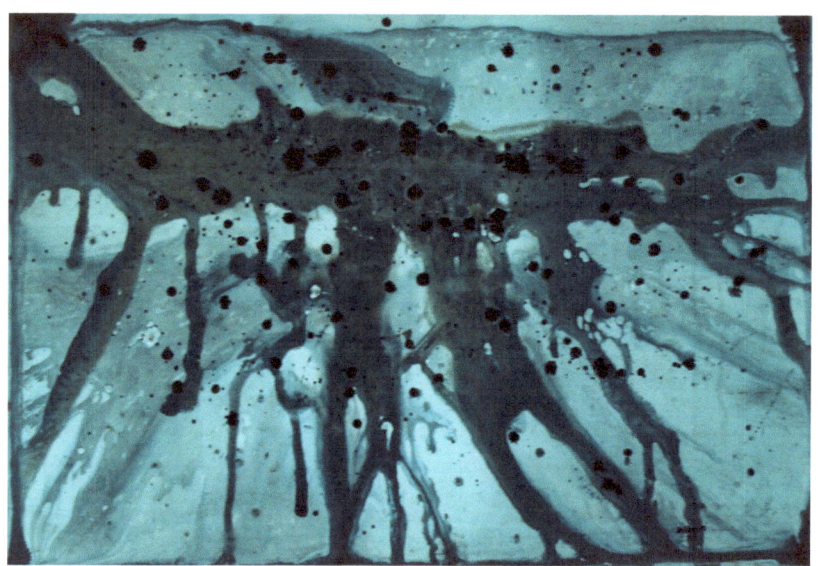

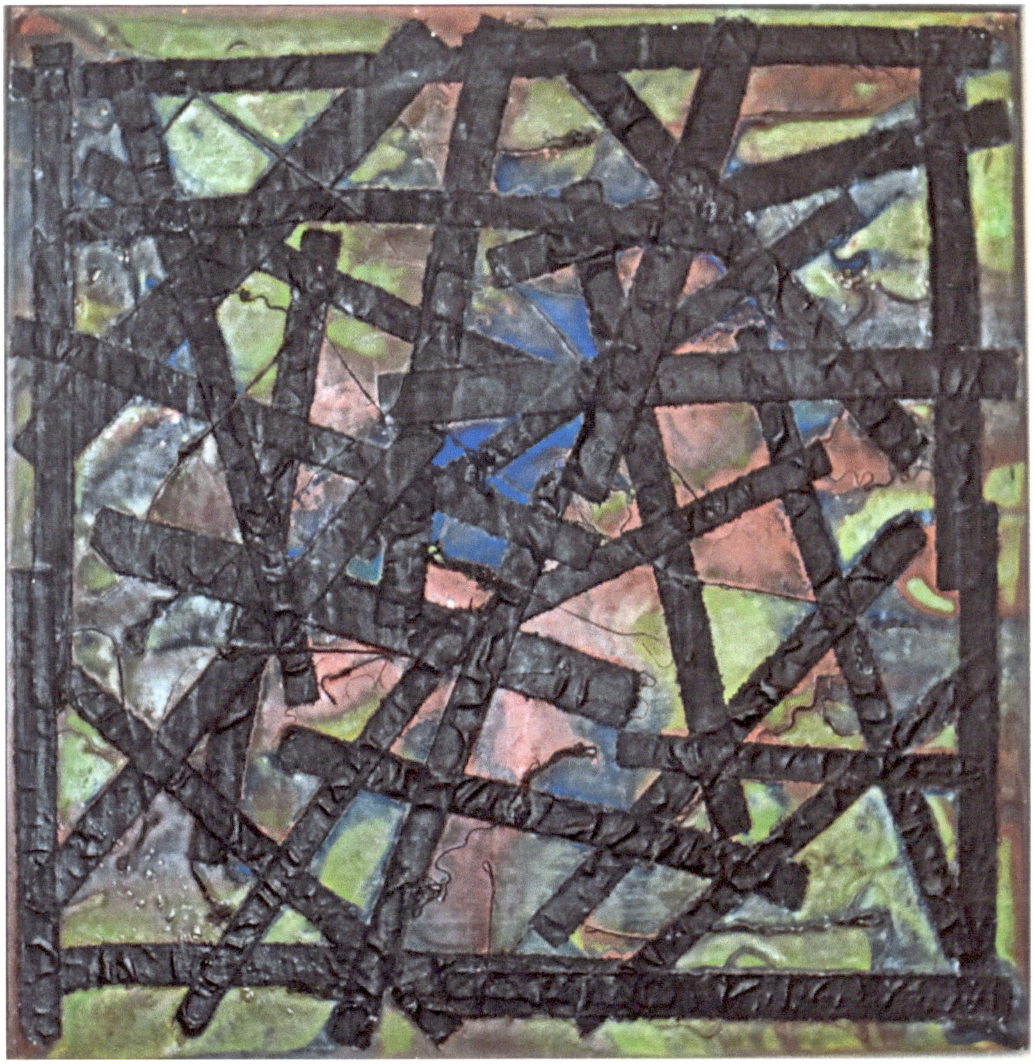

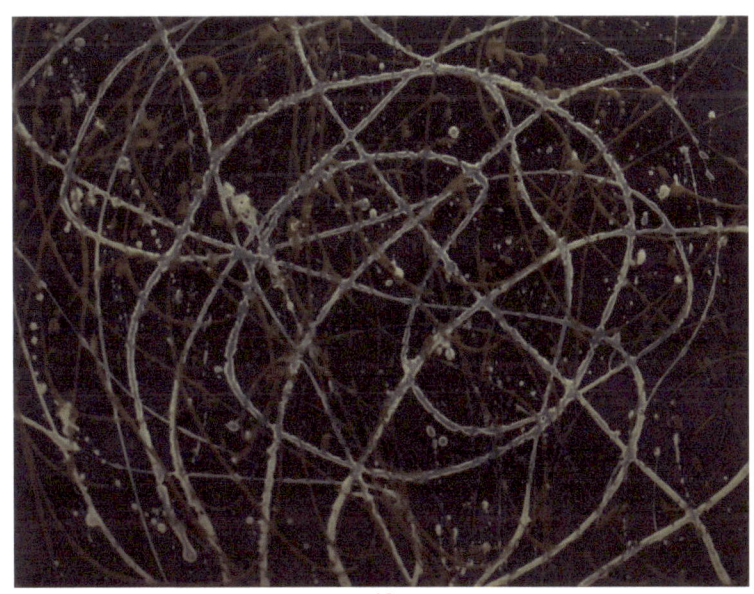

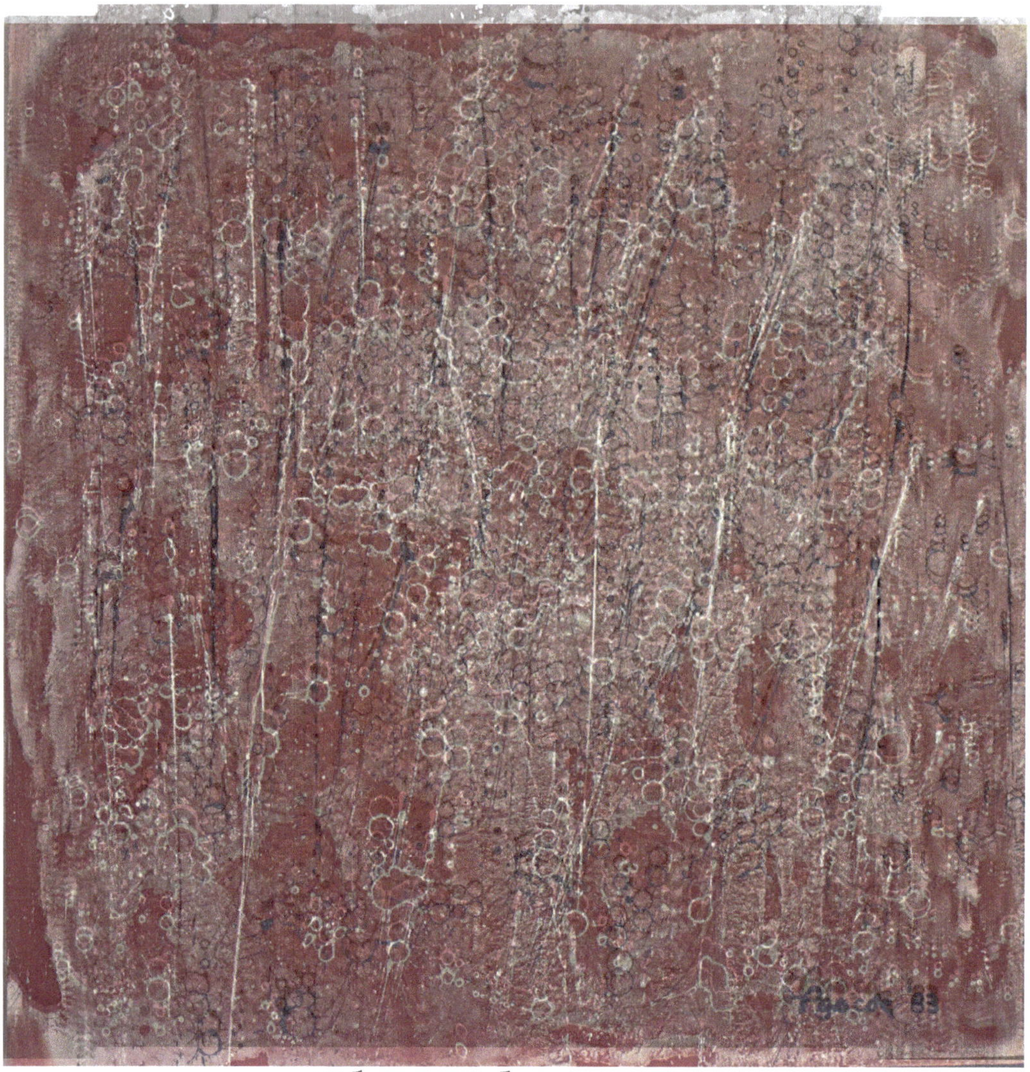

The early 2000s

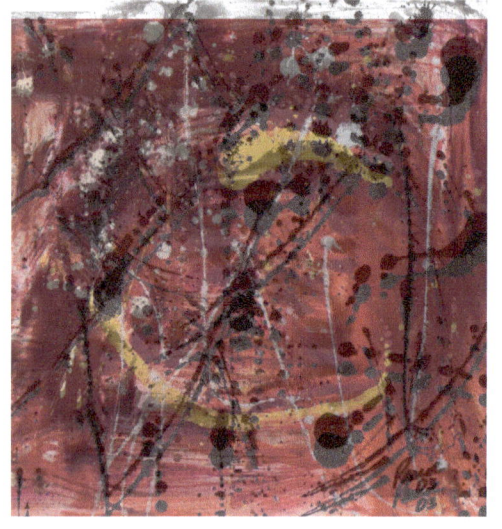
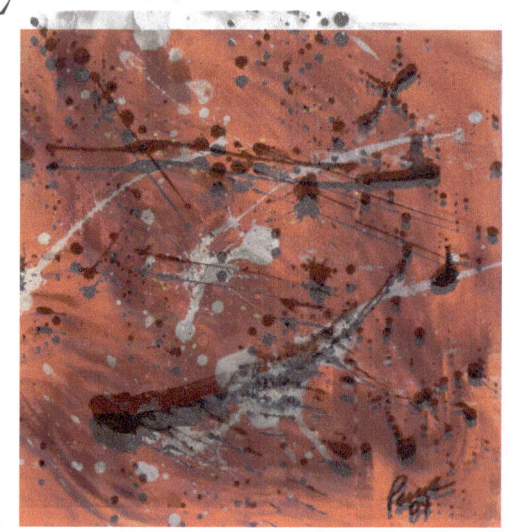

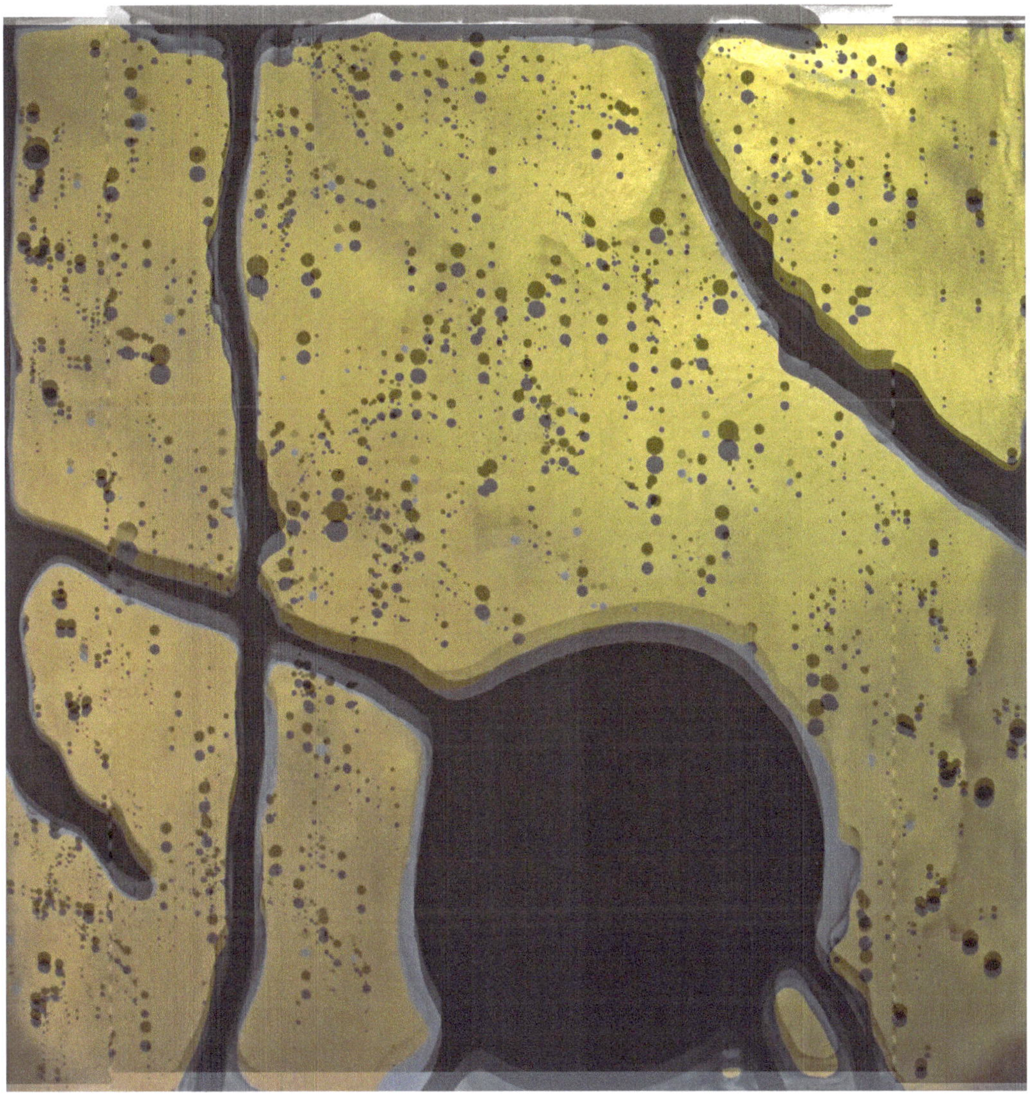

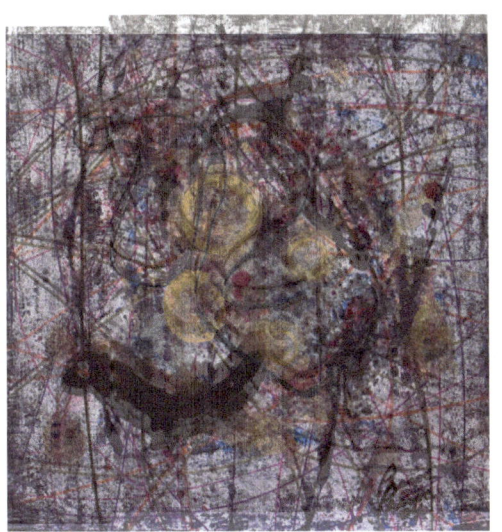
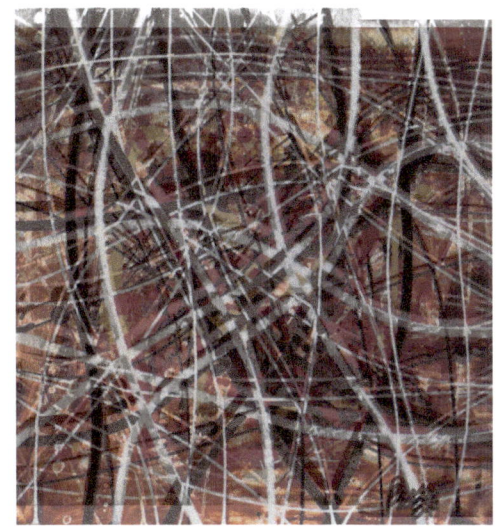

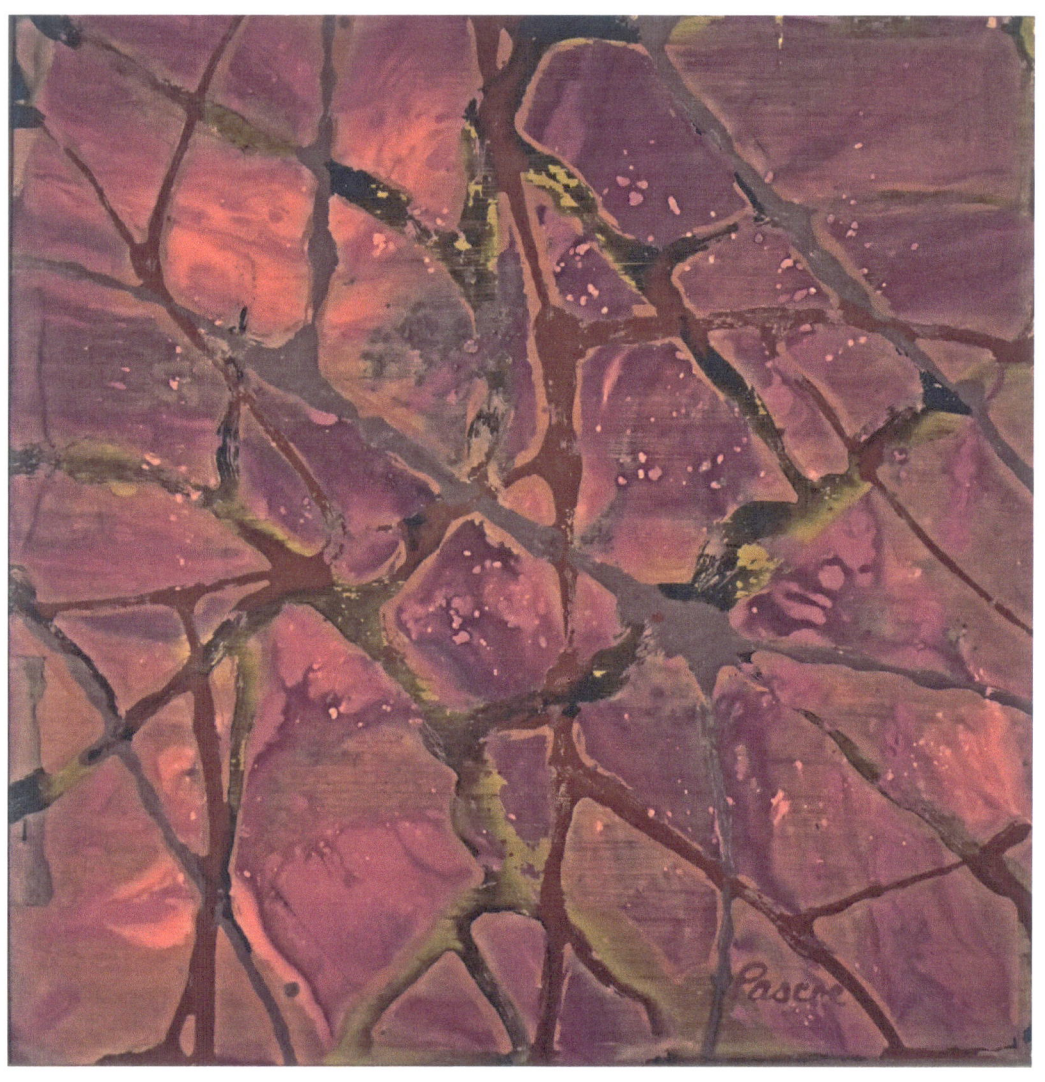
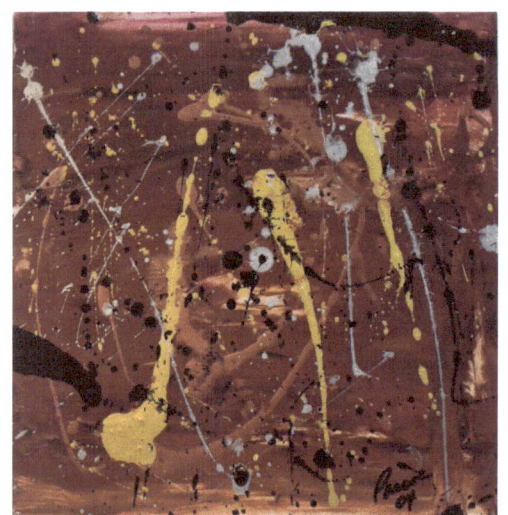
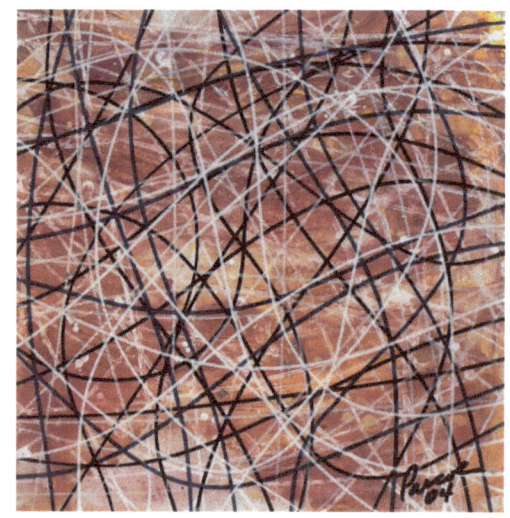

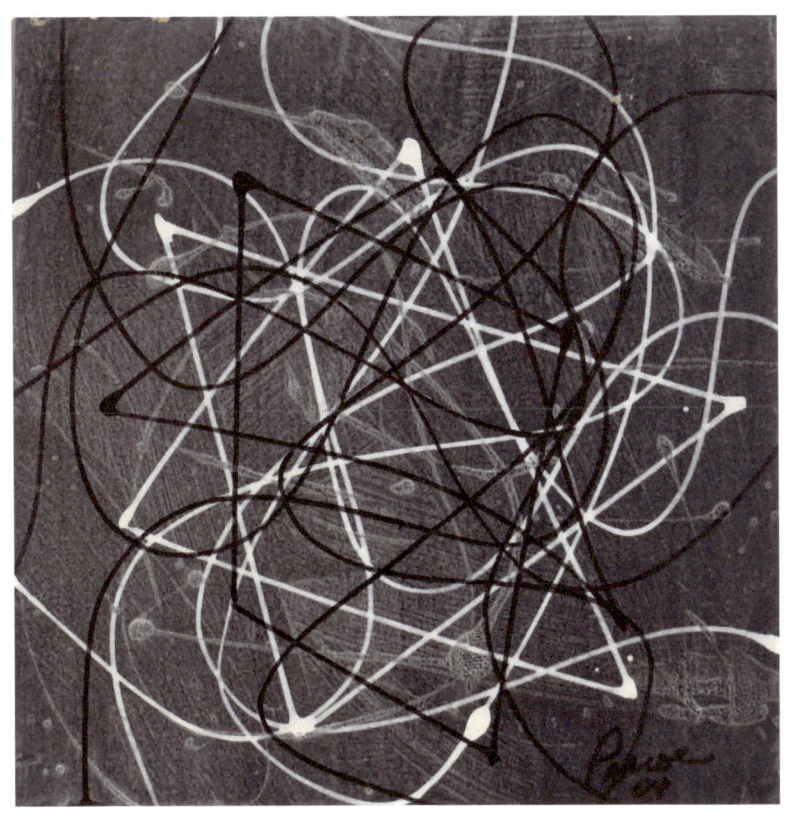

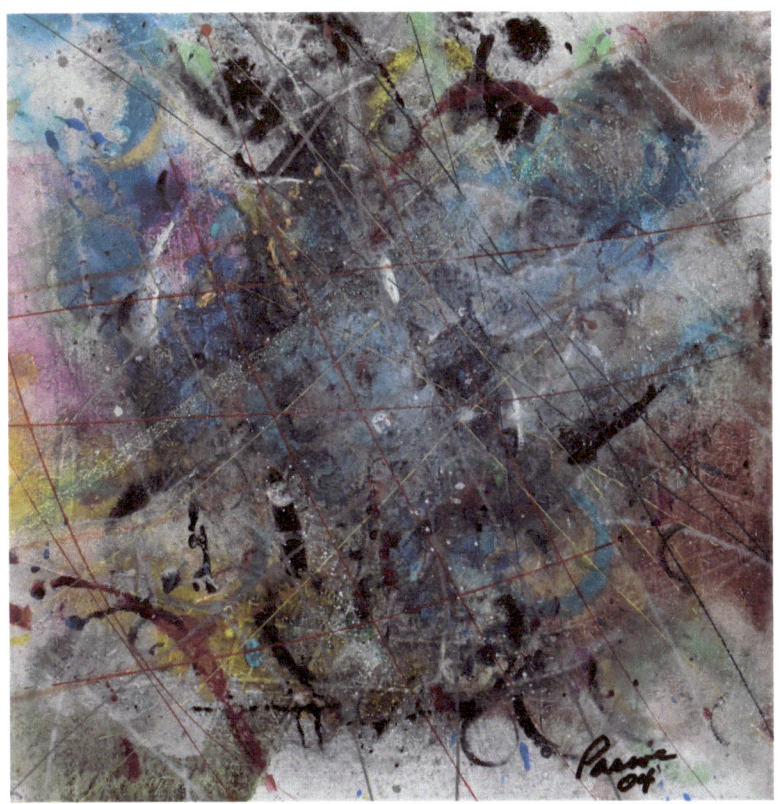

2005

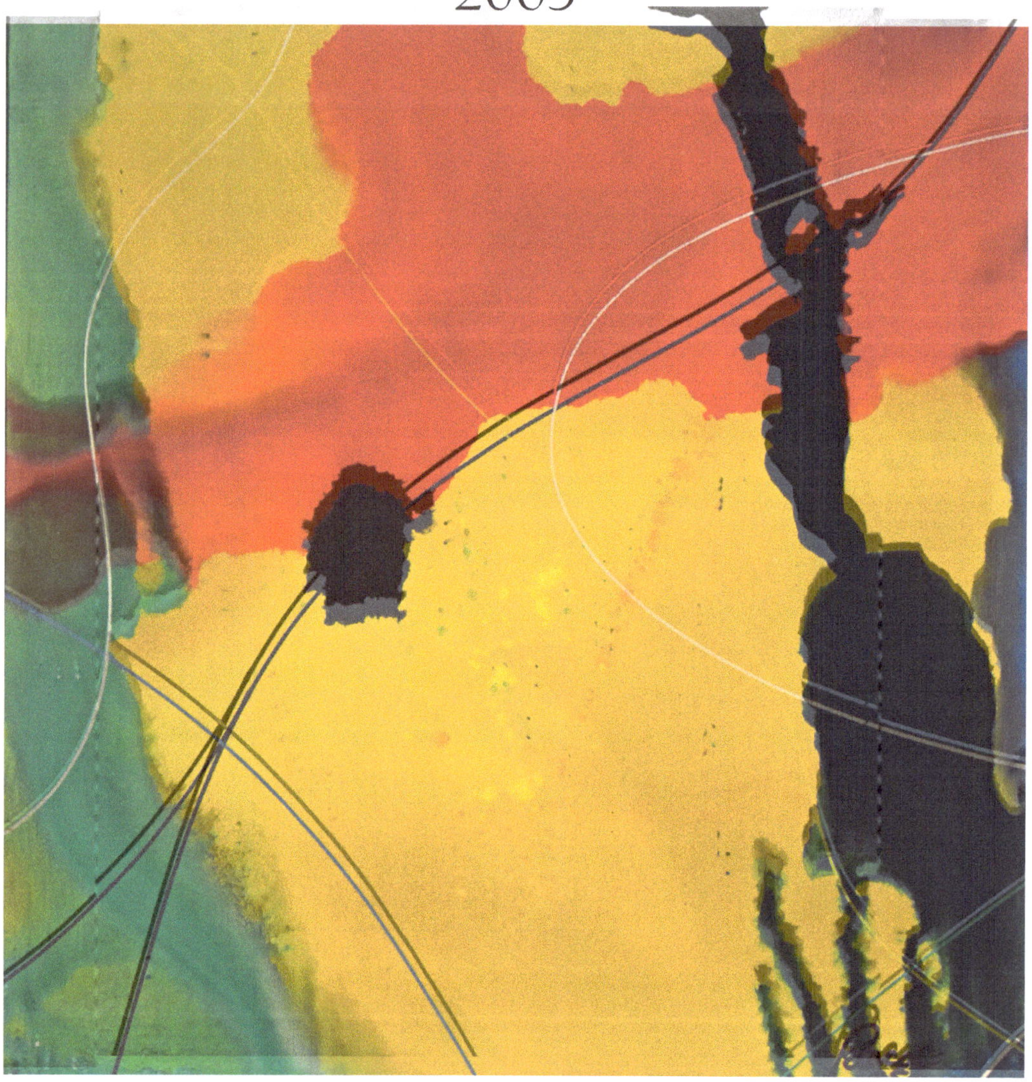

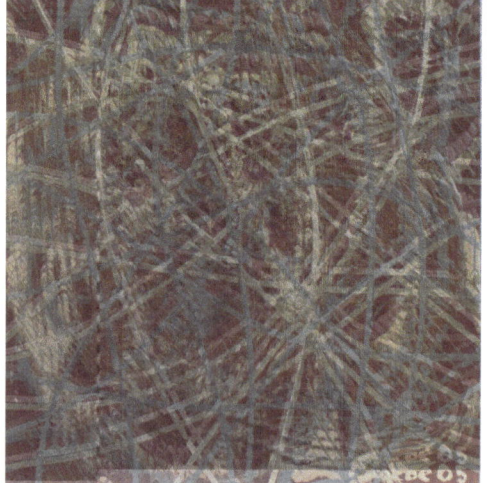
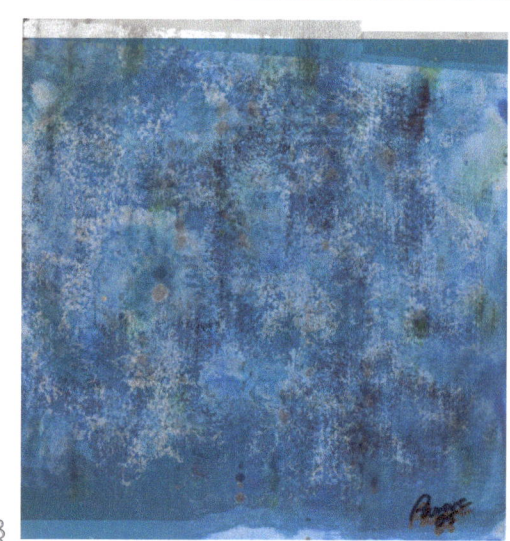

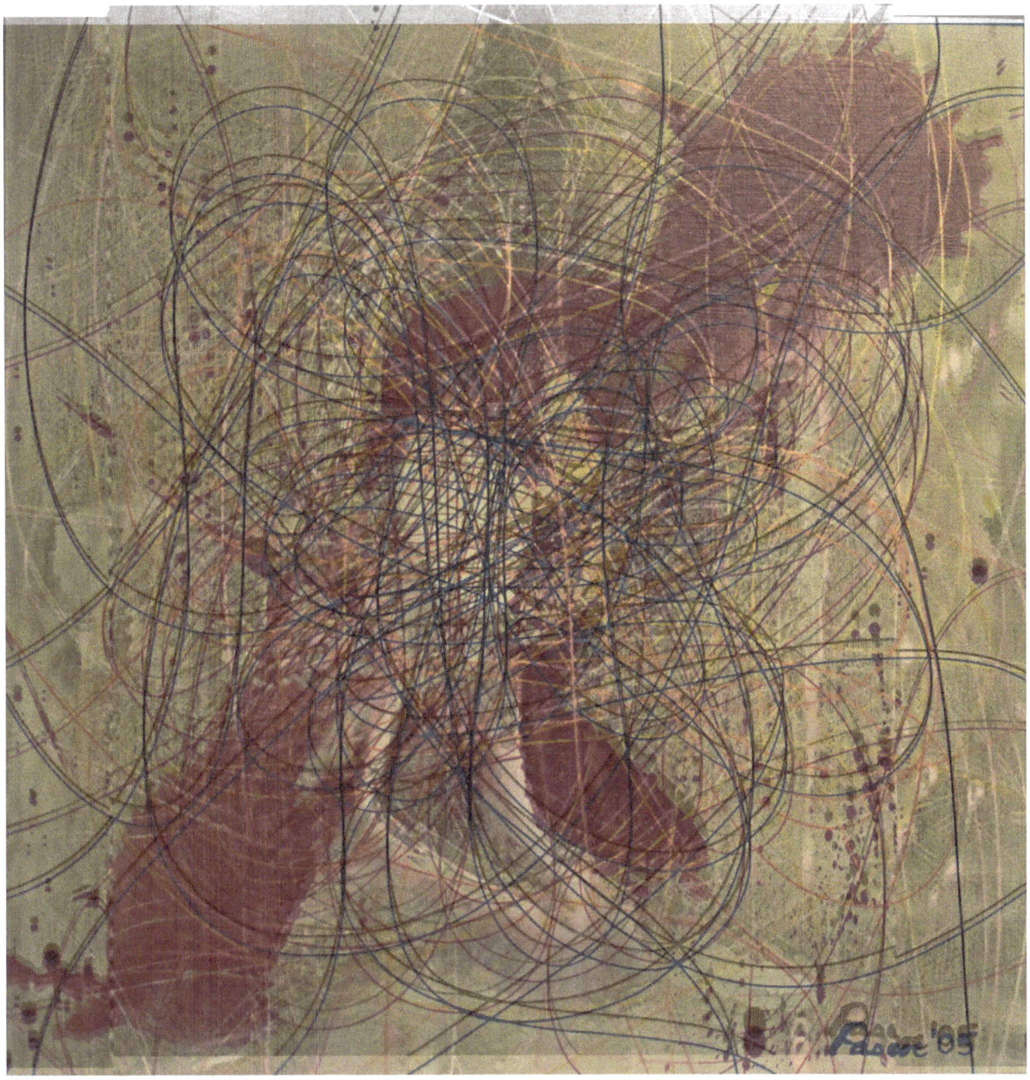

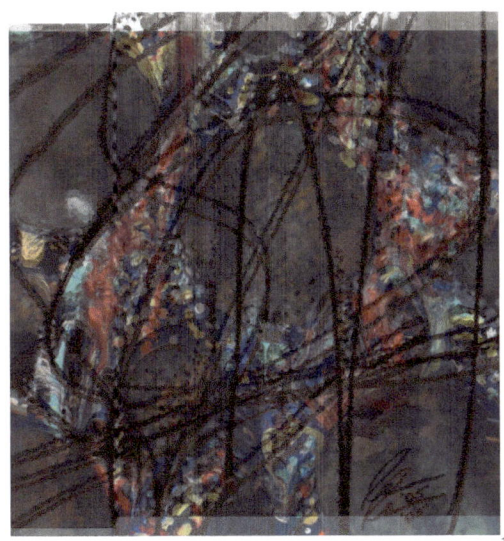
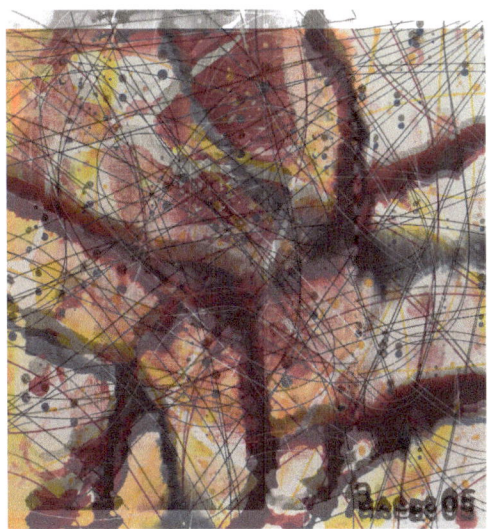

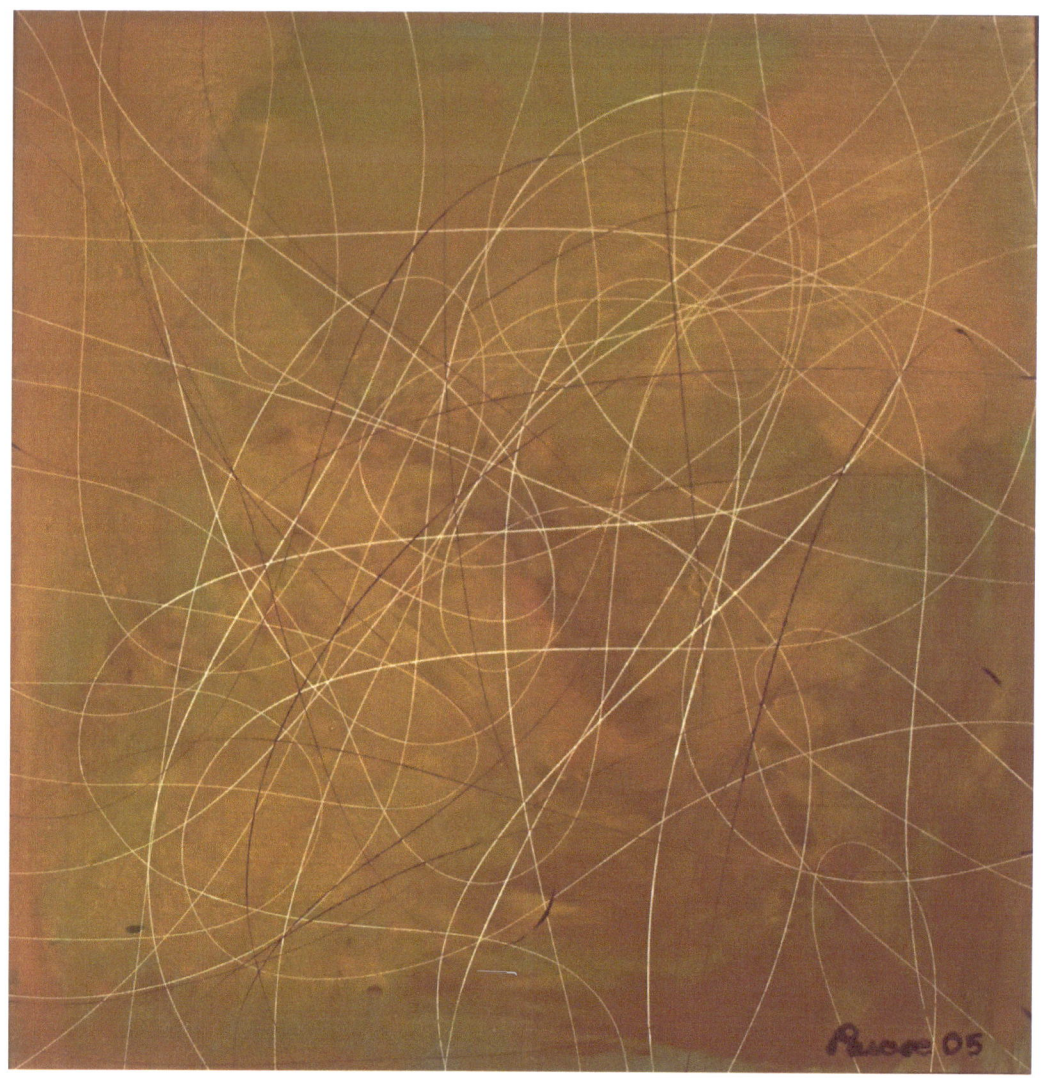
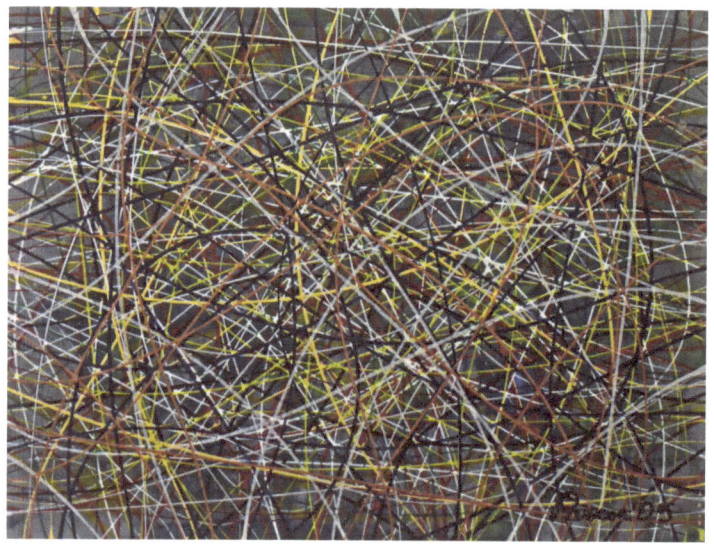

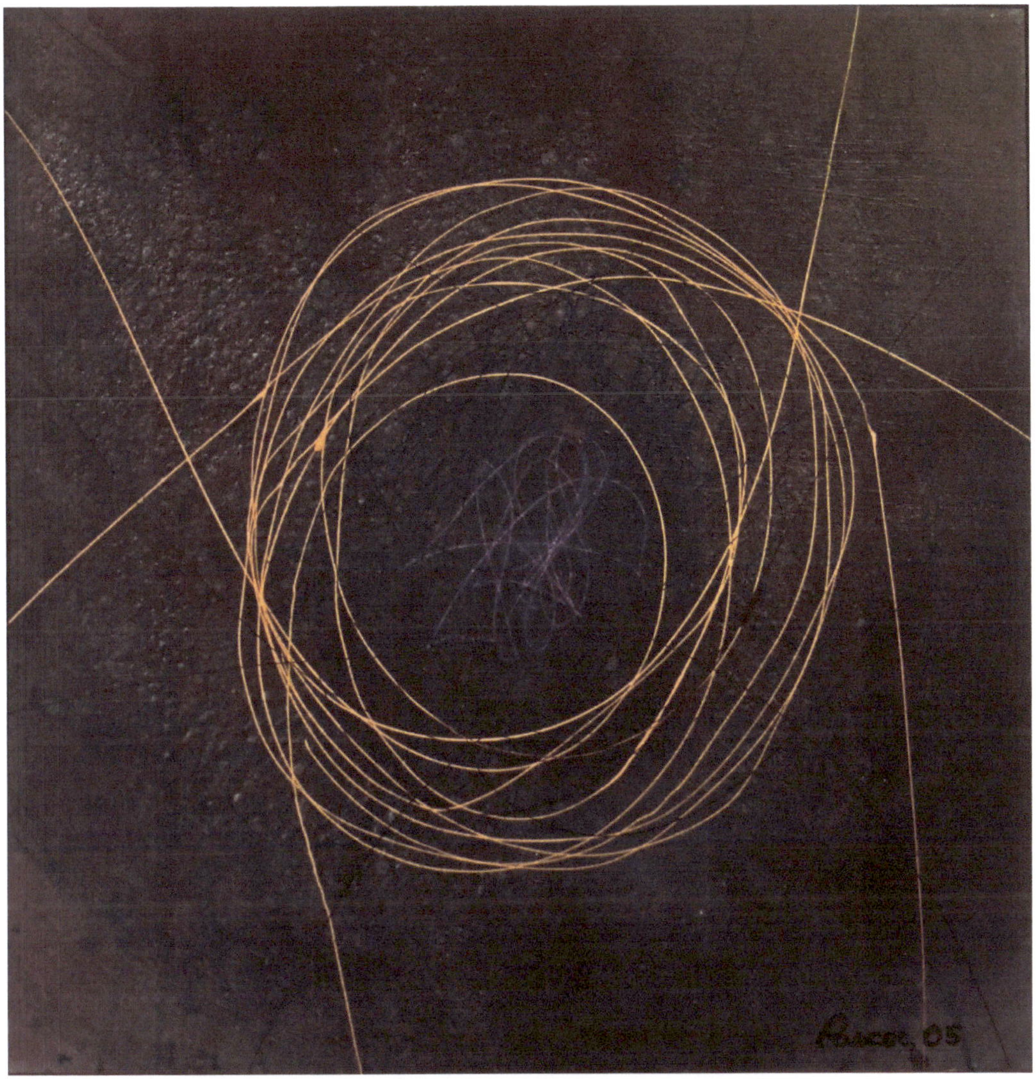

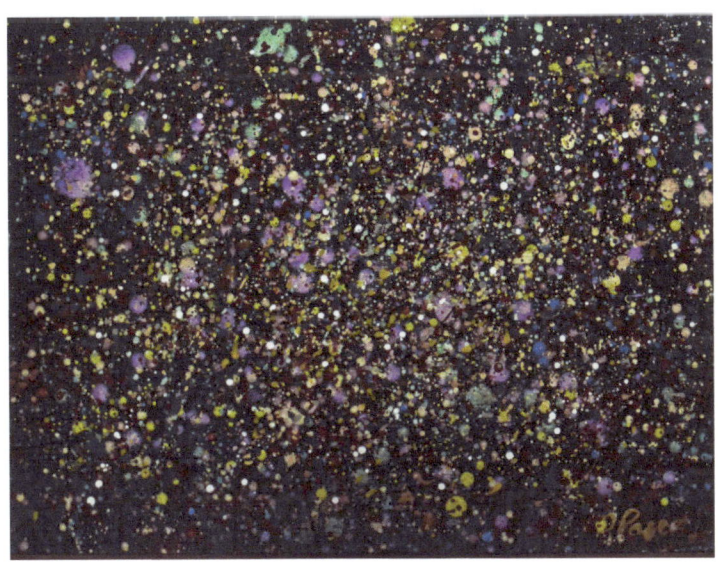

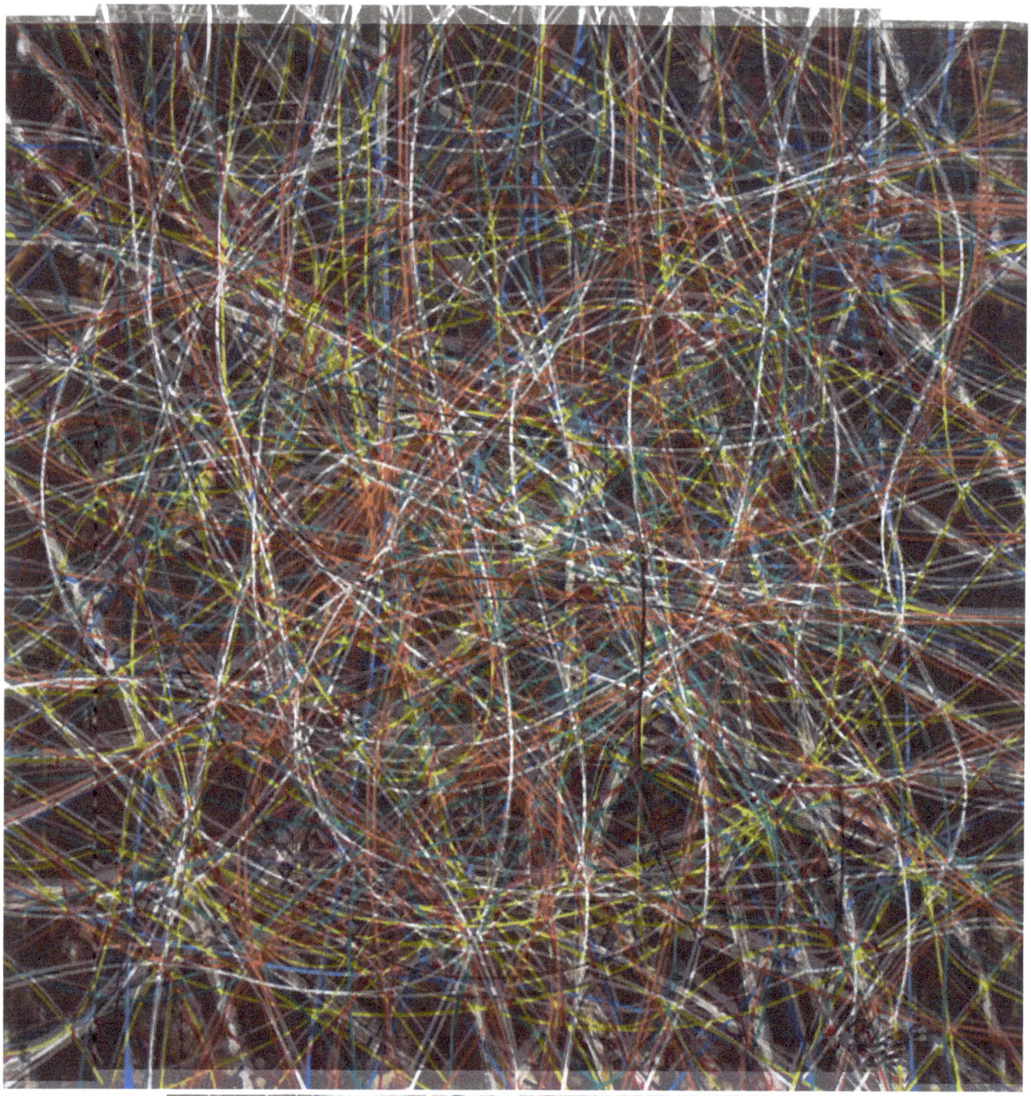

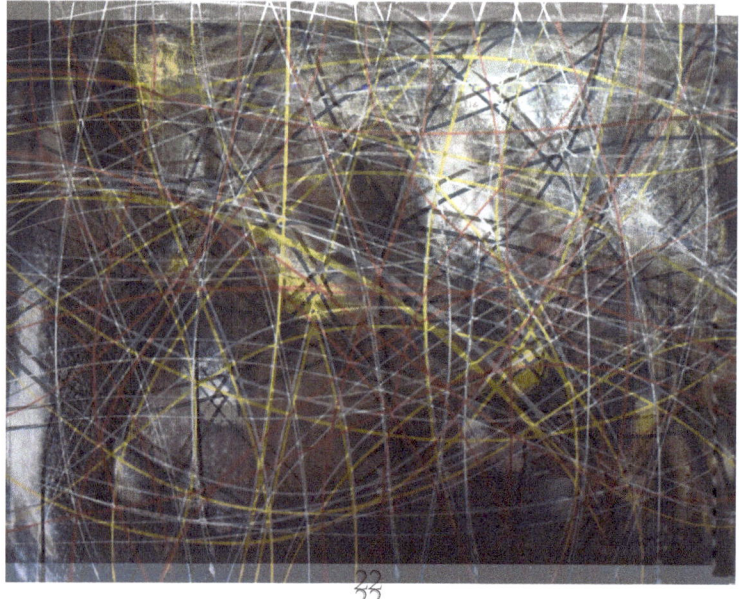

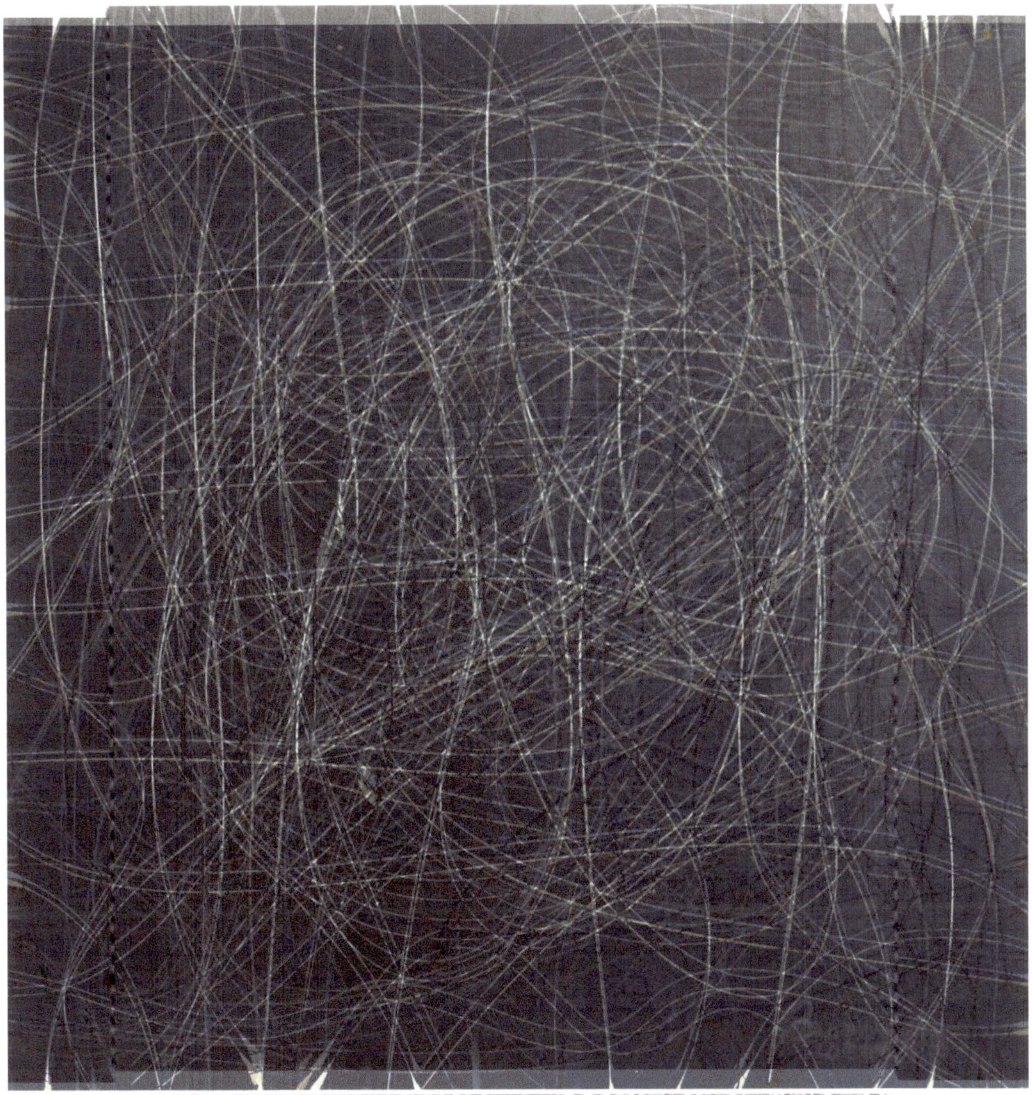

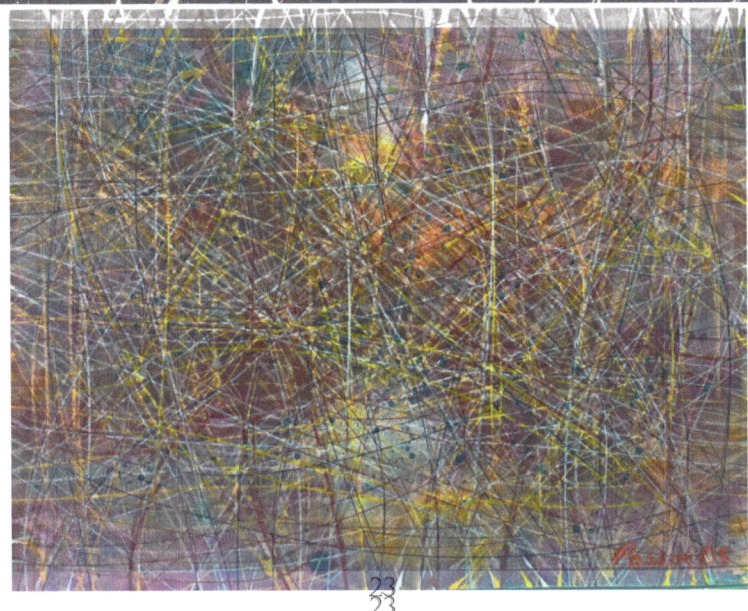

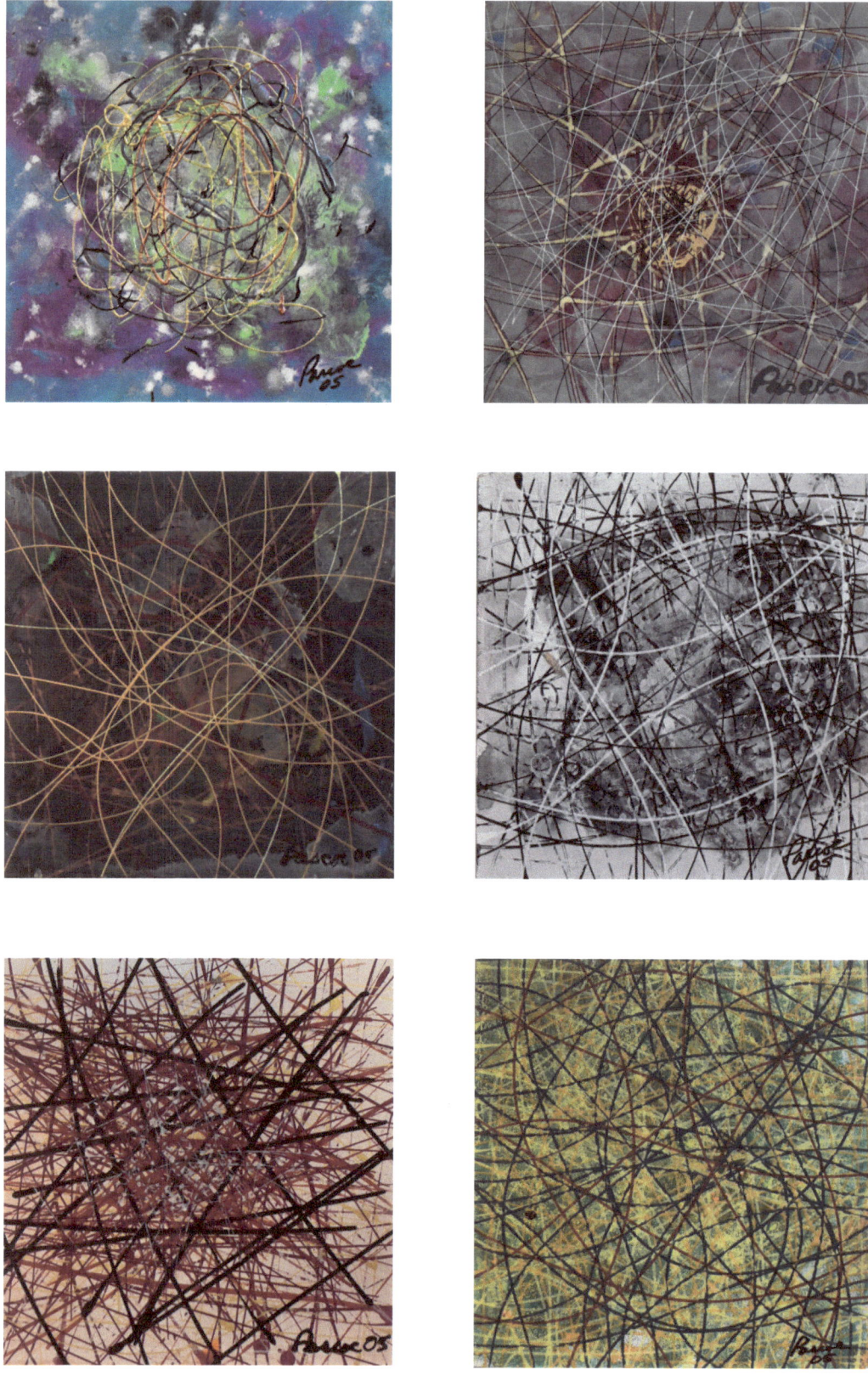

2006

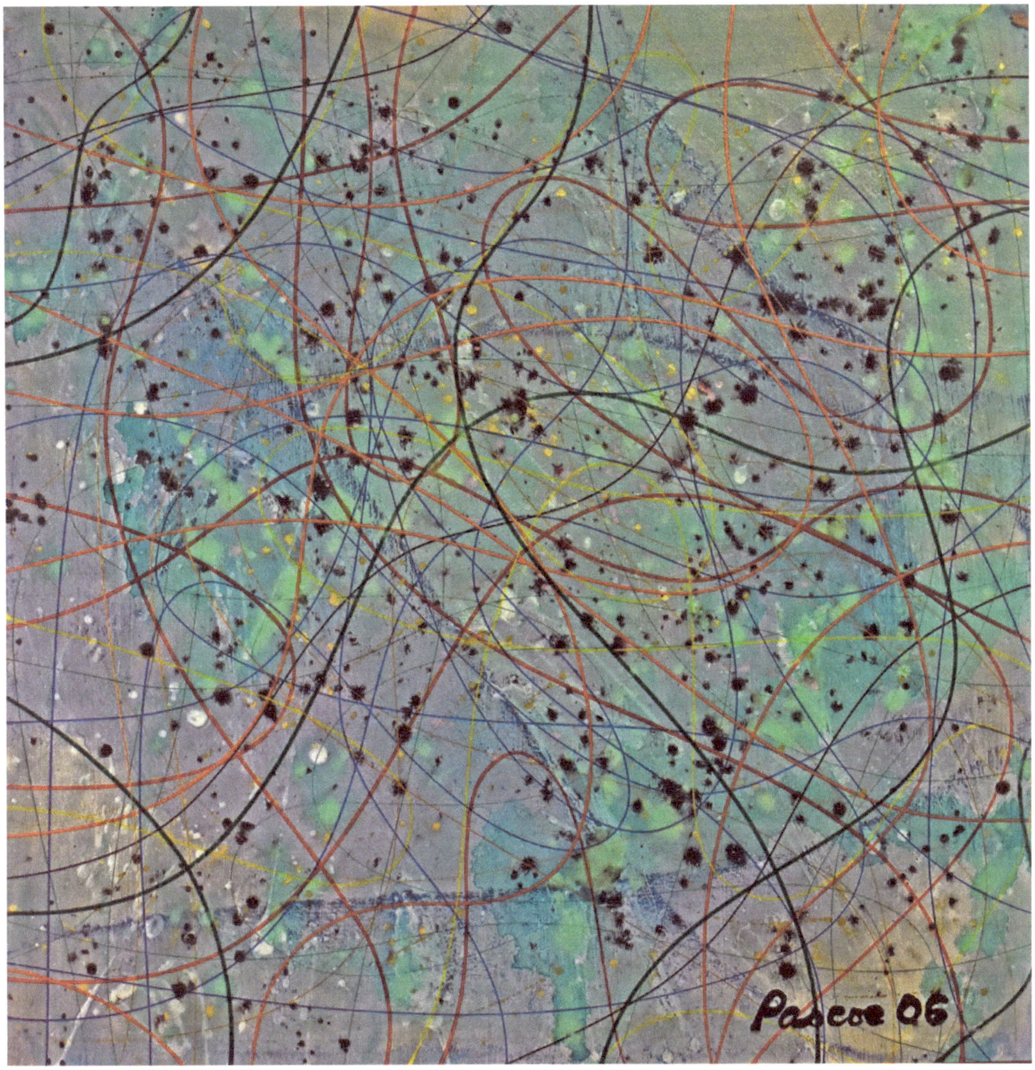

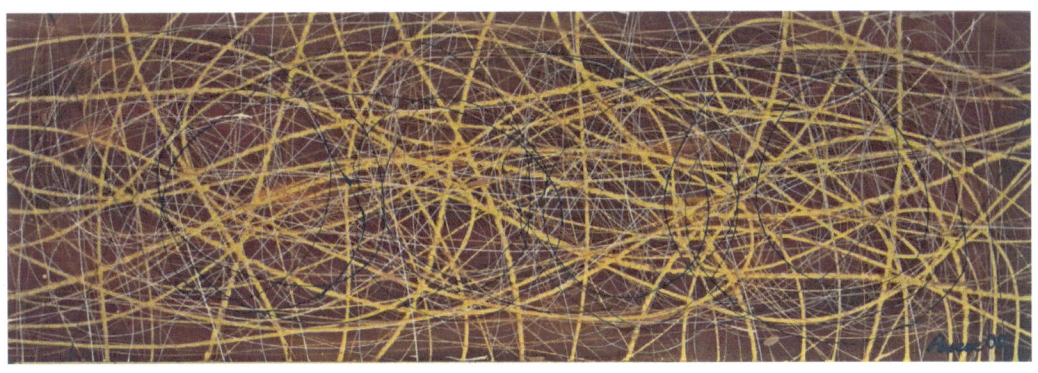

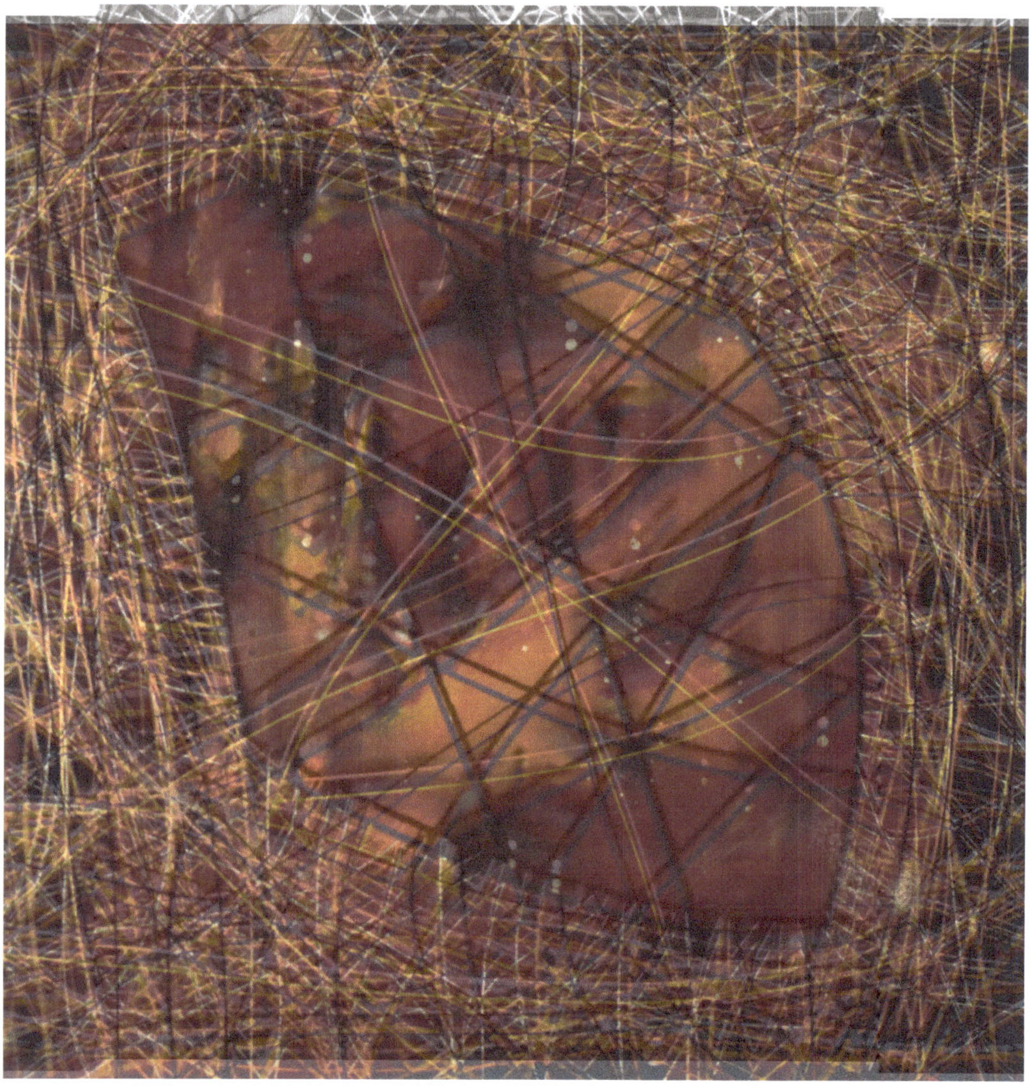

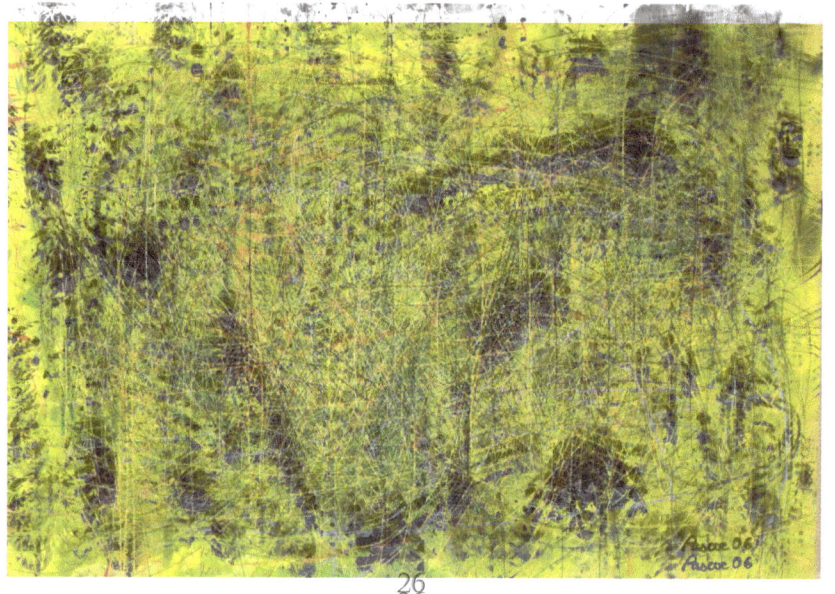

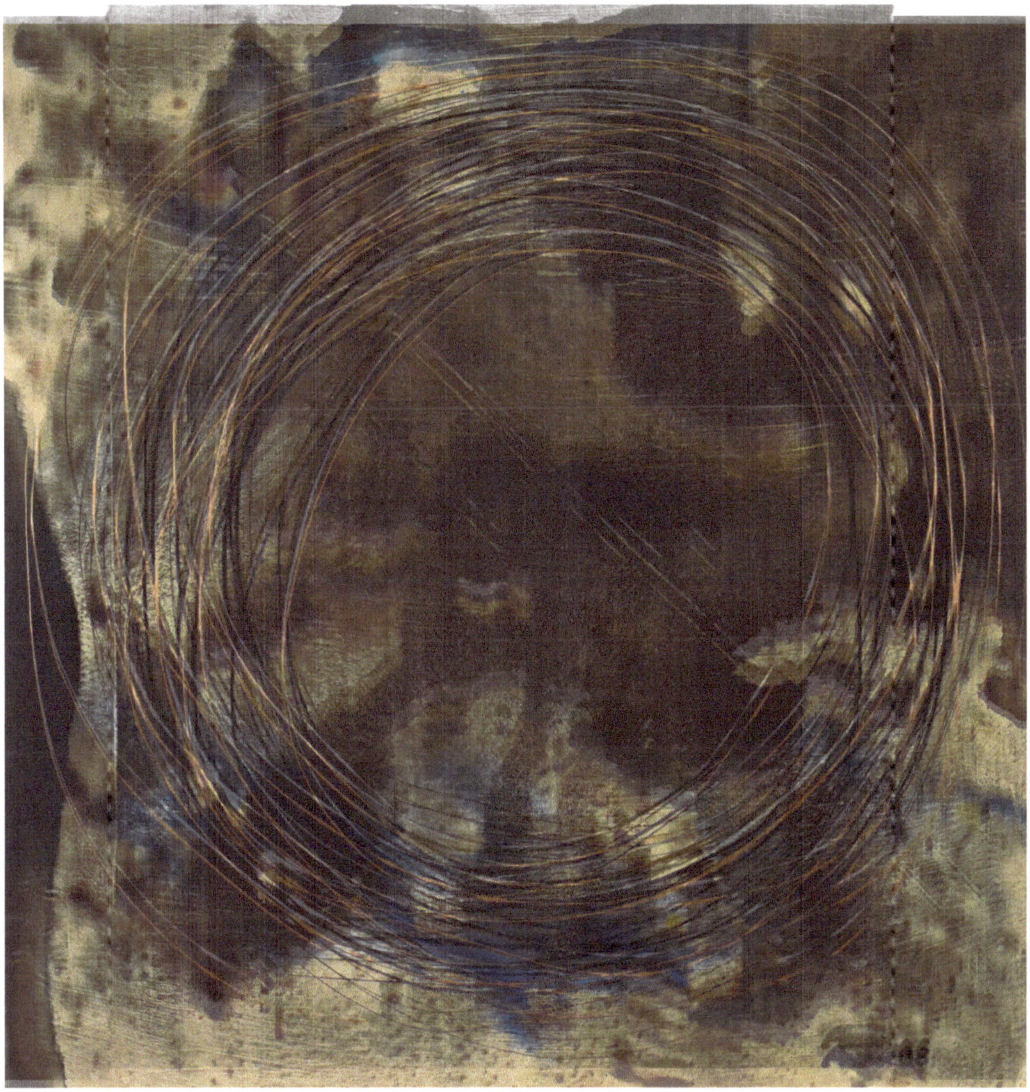

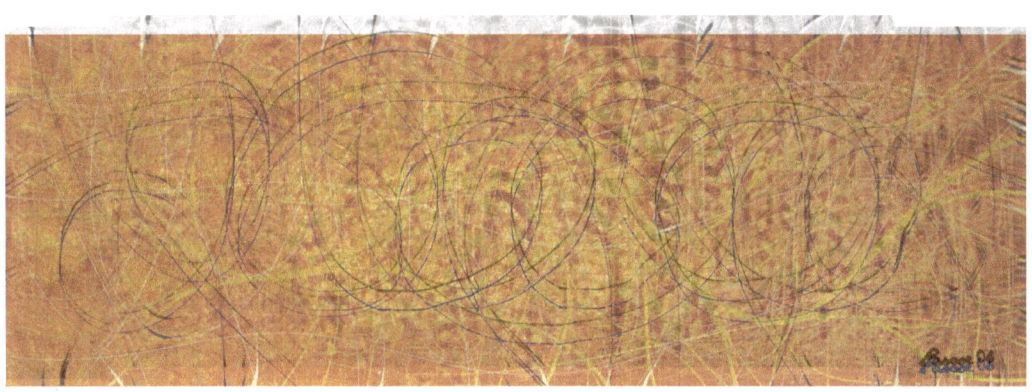

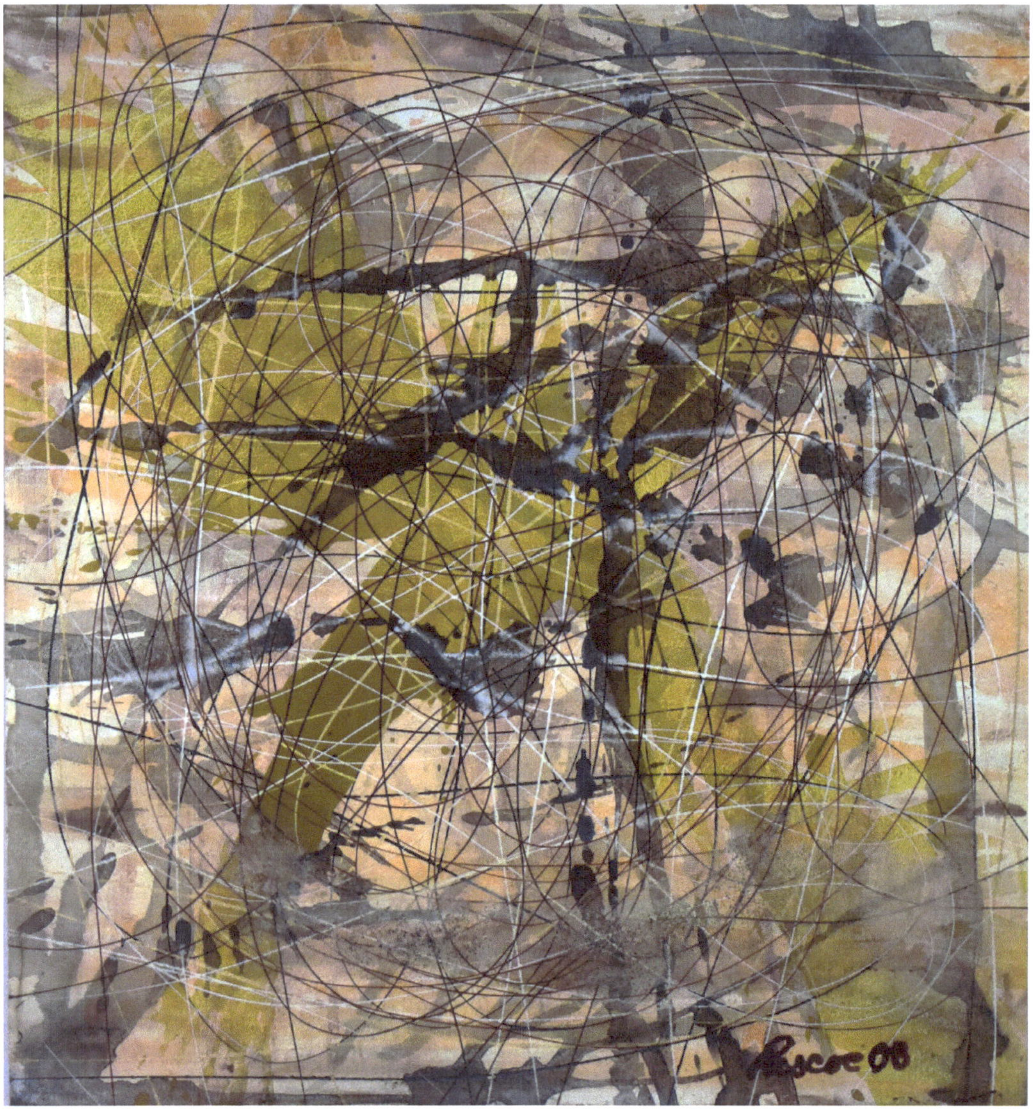

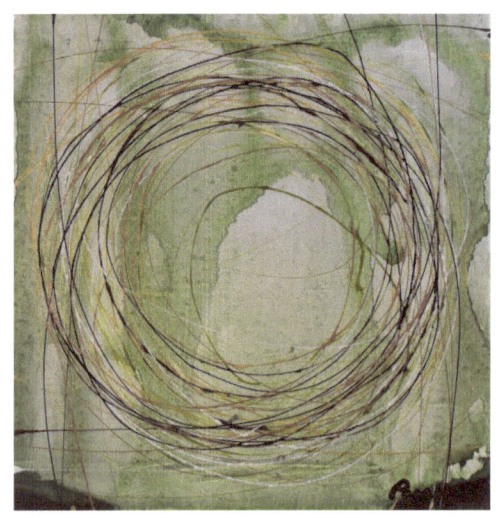
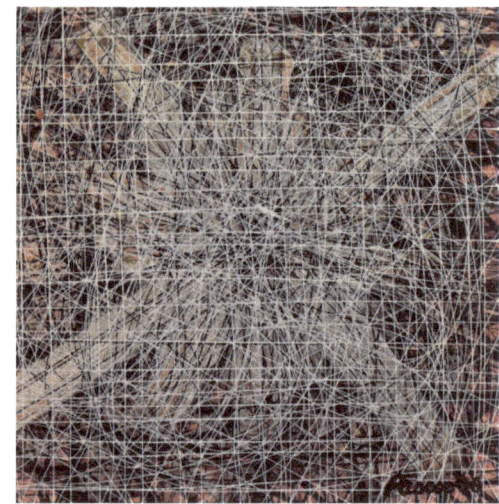

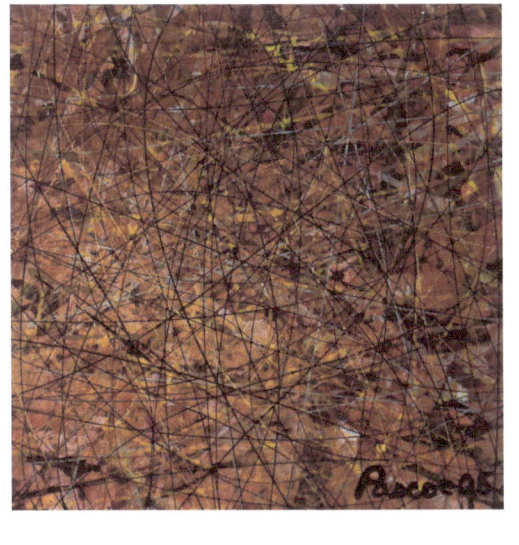
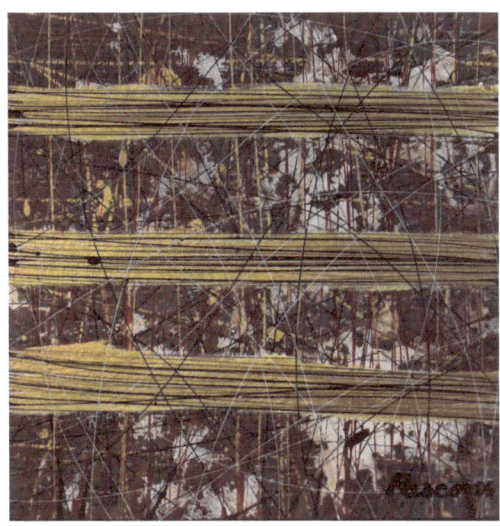
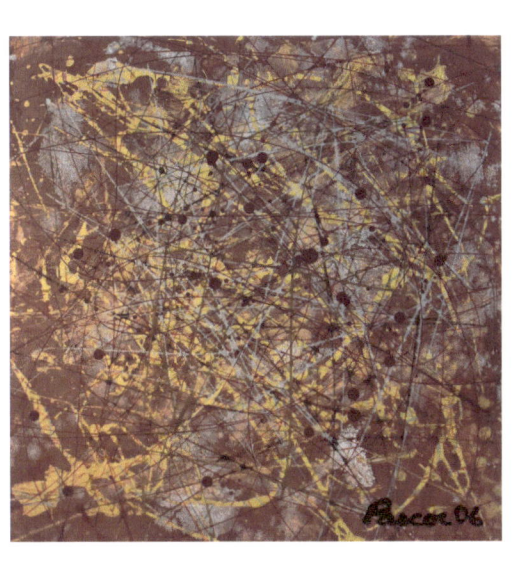
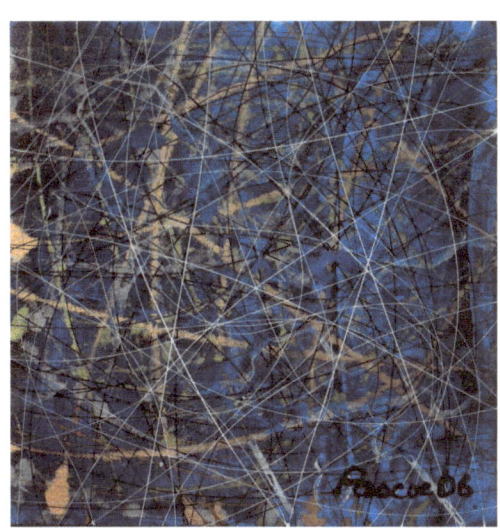
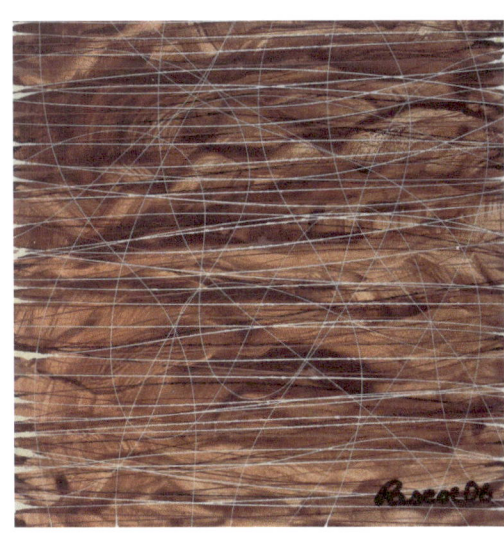
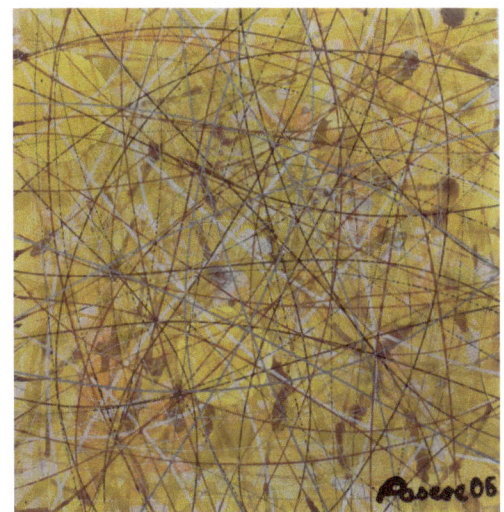

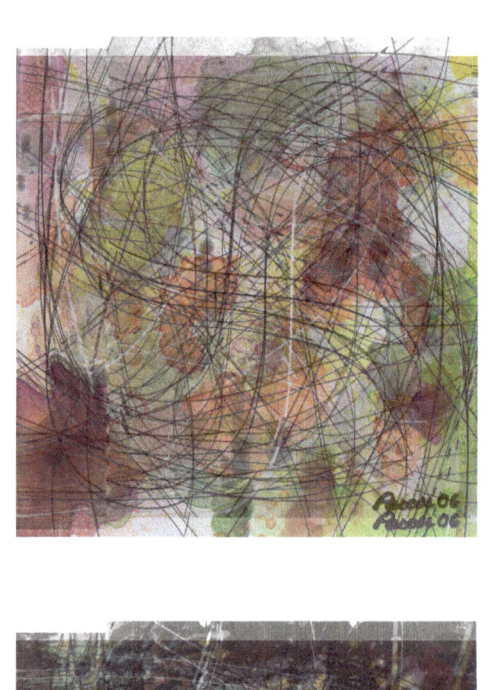
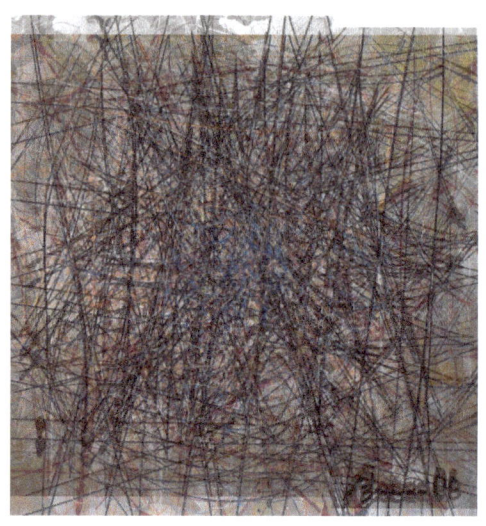
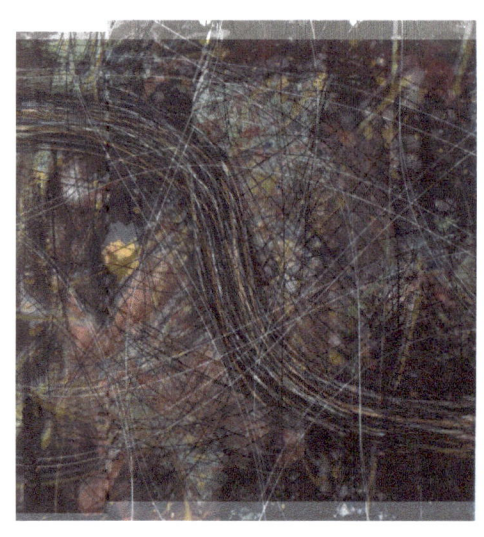
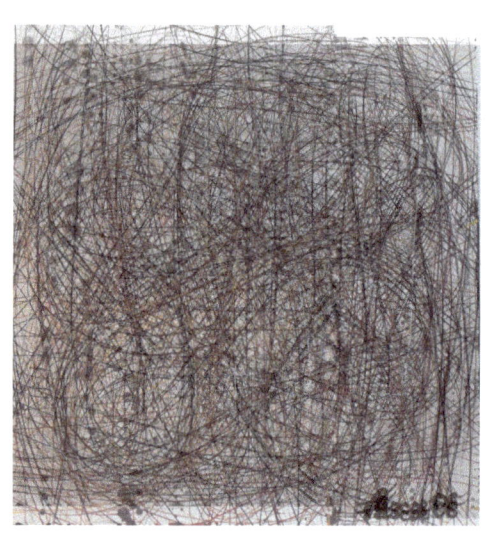
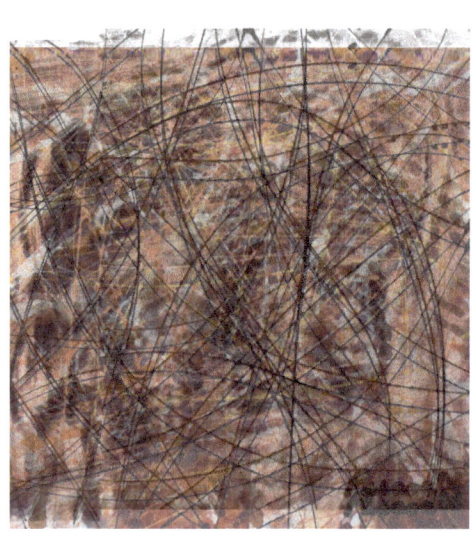
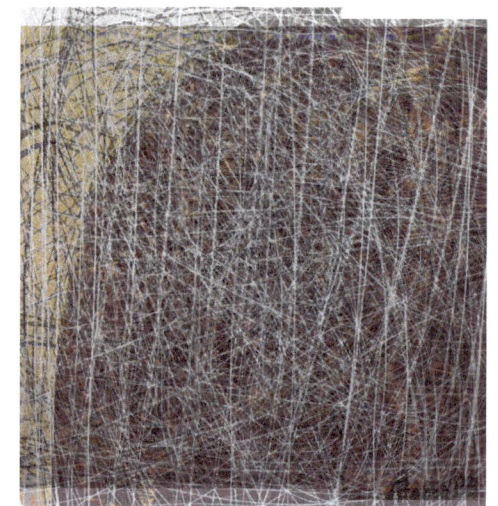

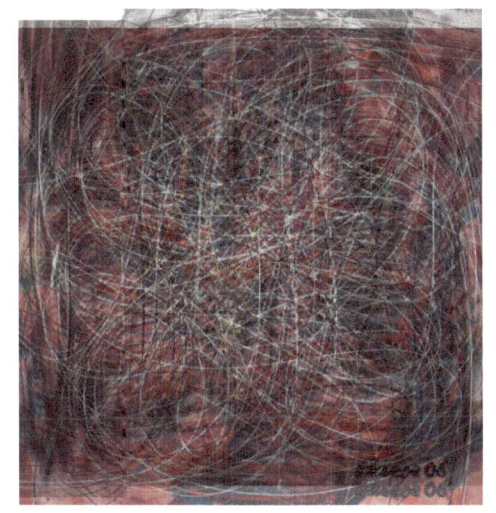 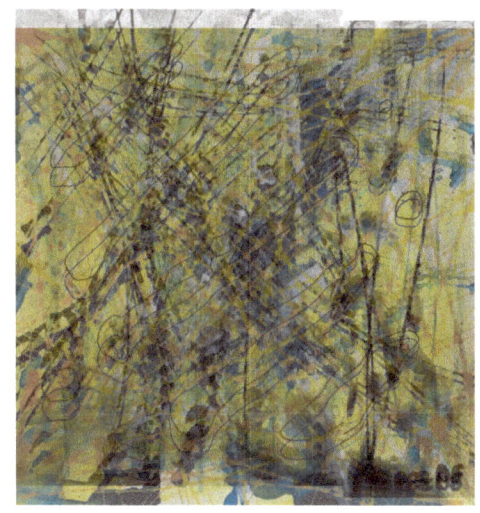

2007

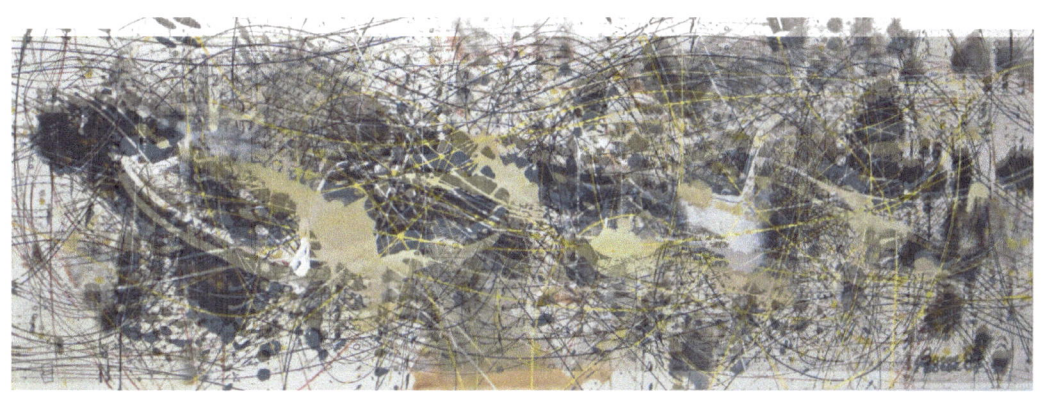

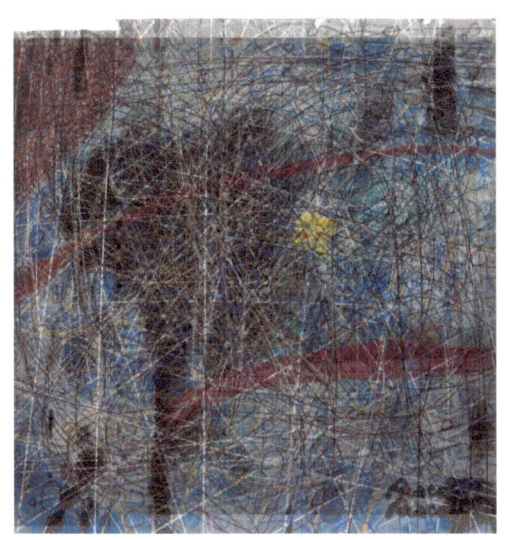 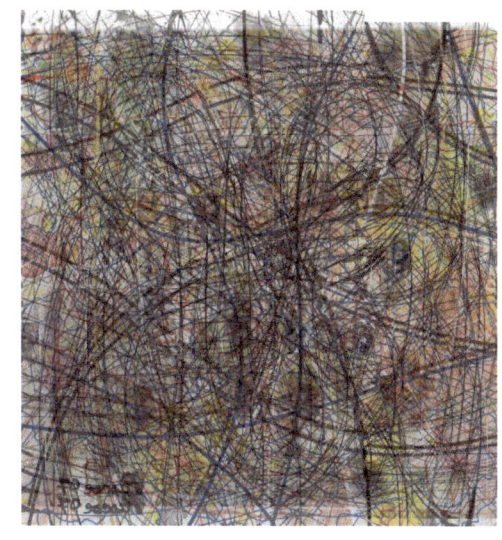

2008

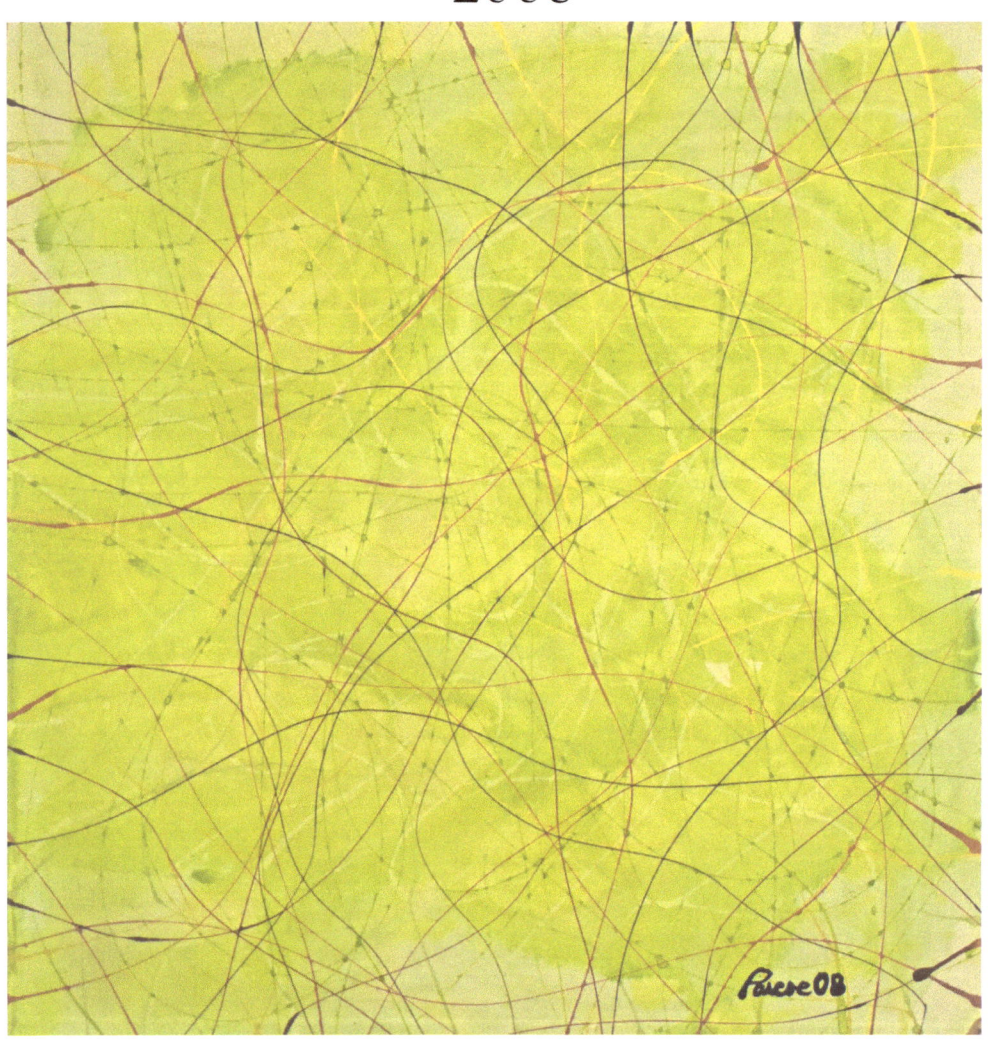

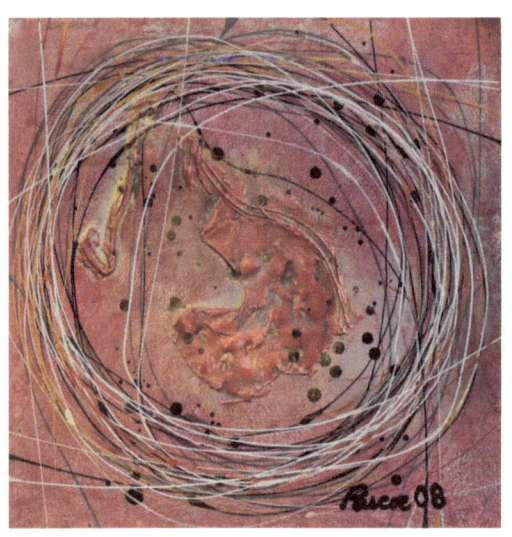

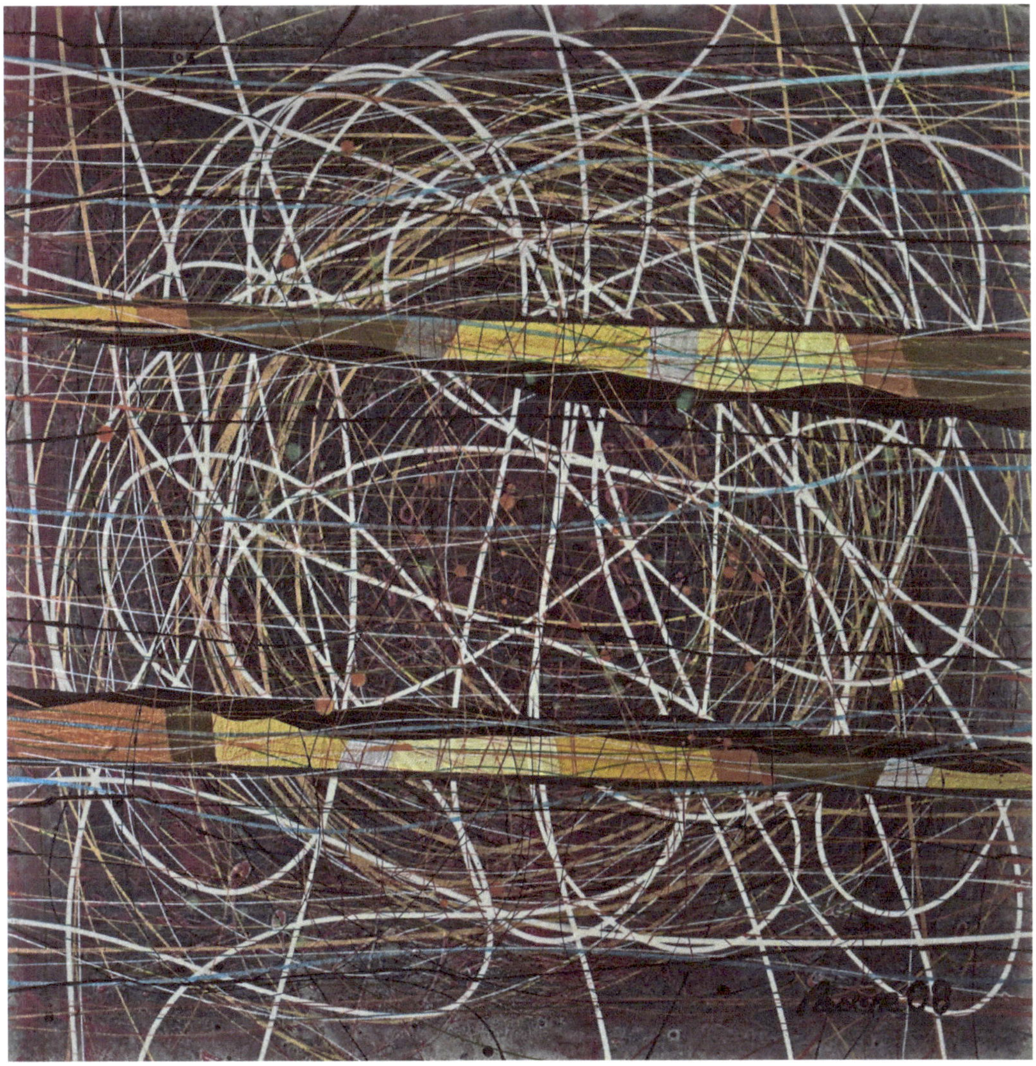

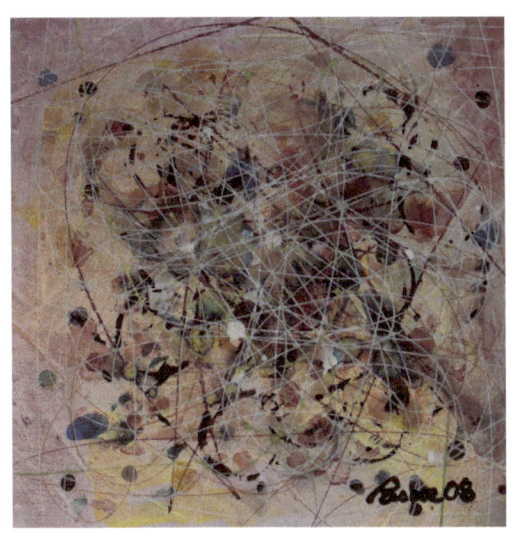

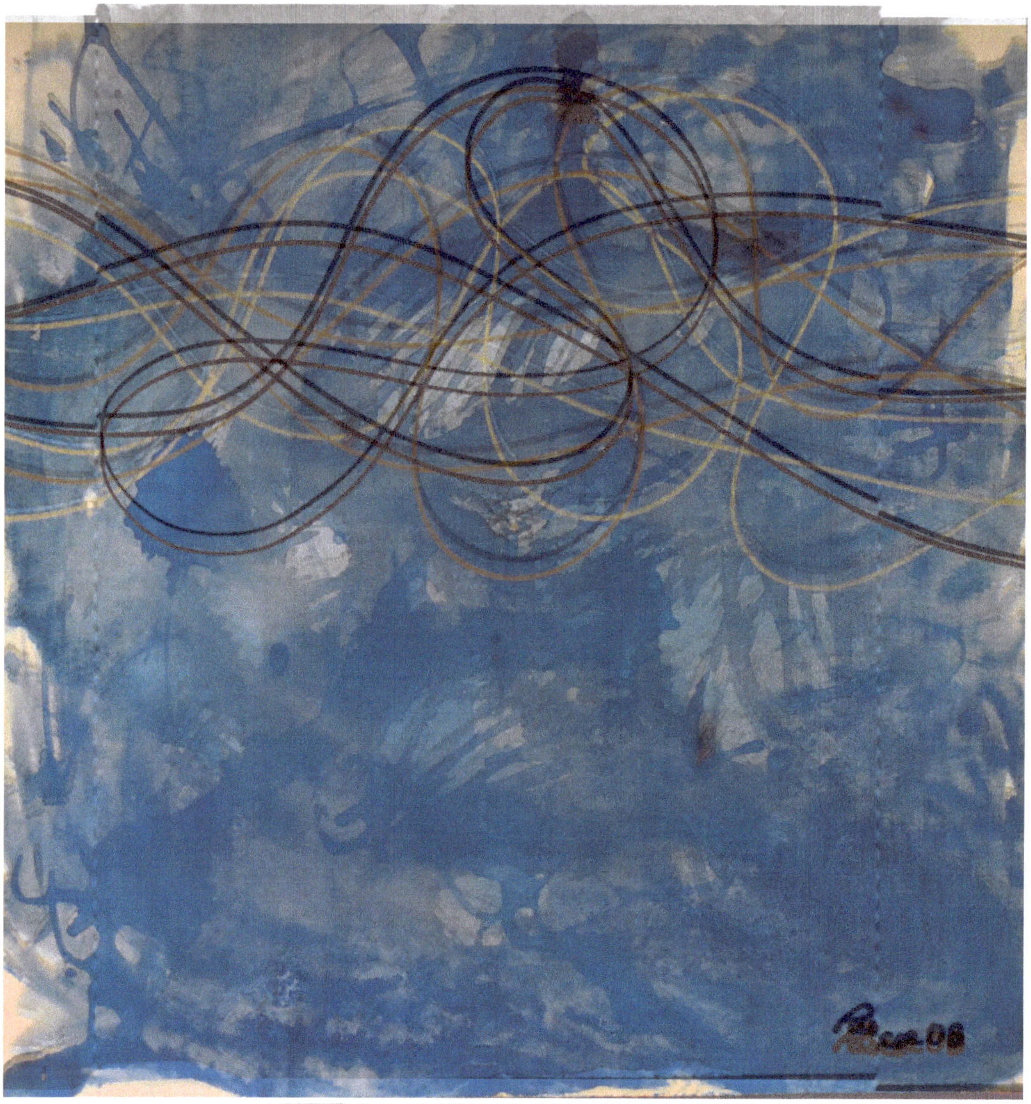

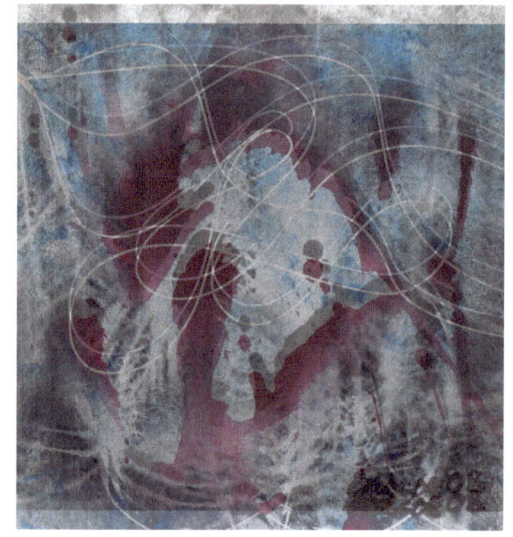

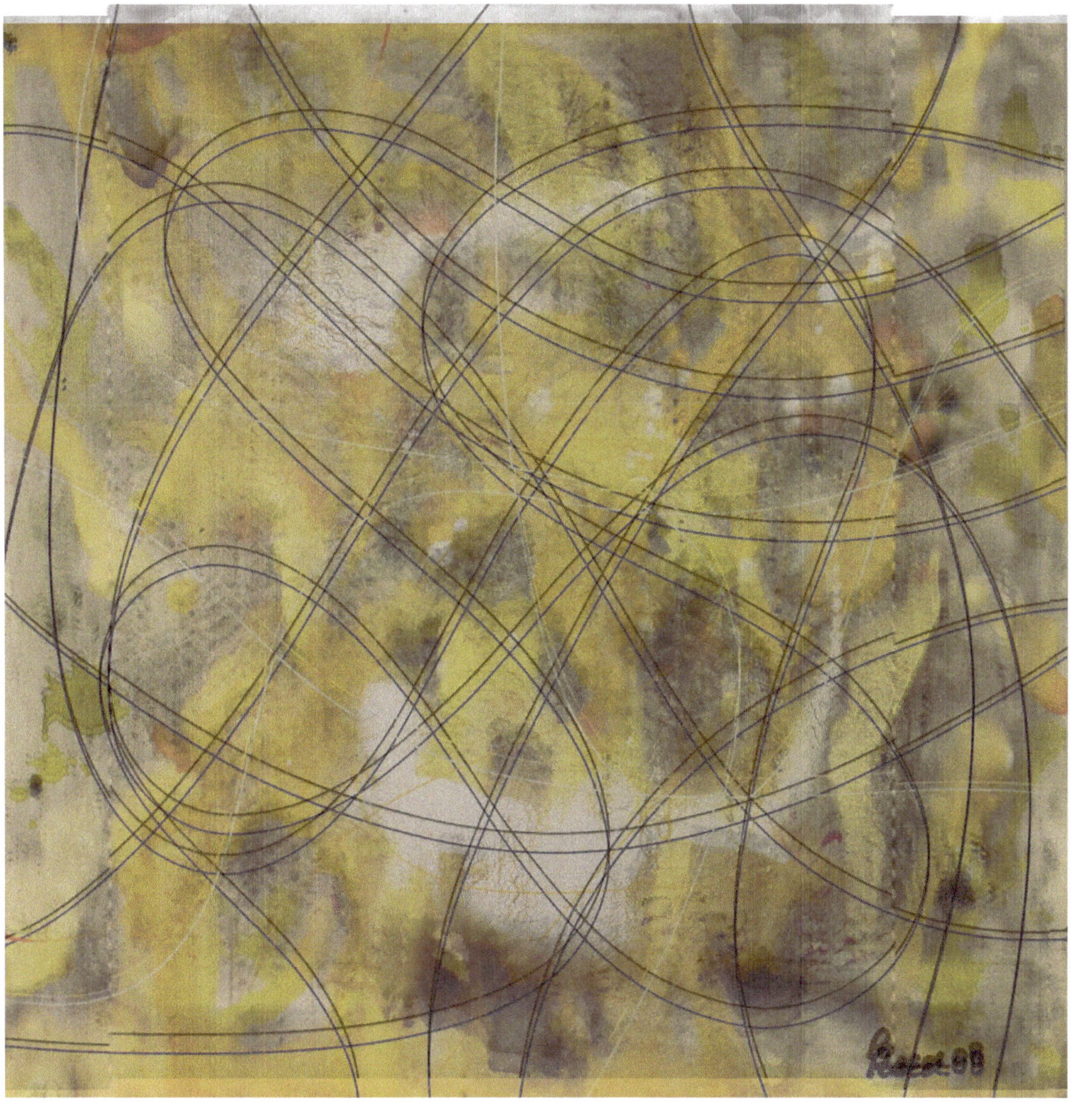

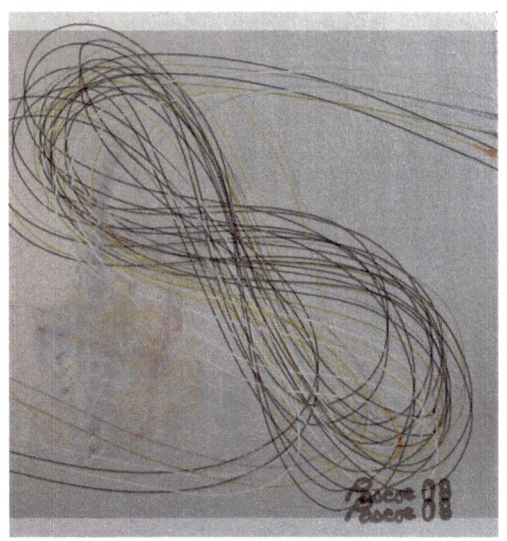

35

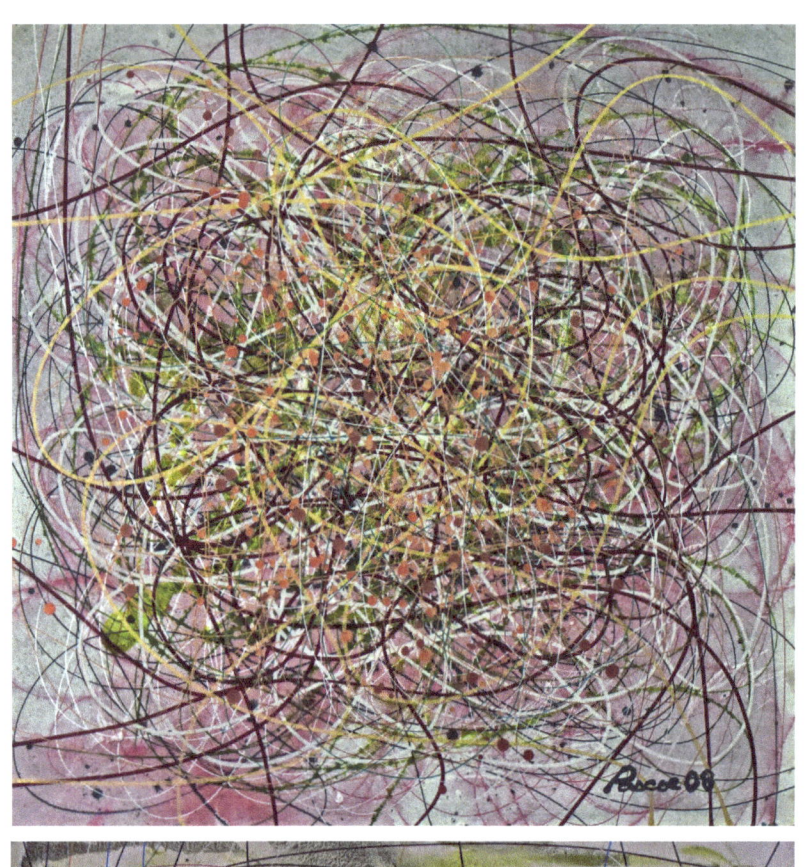

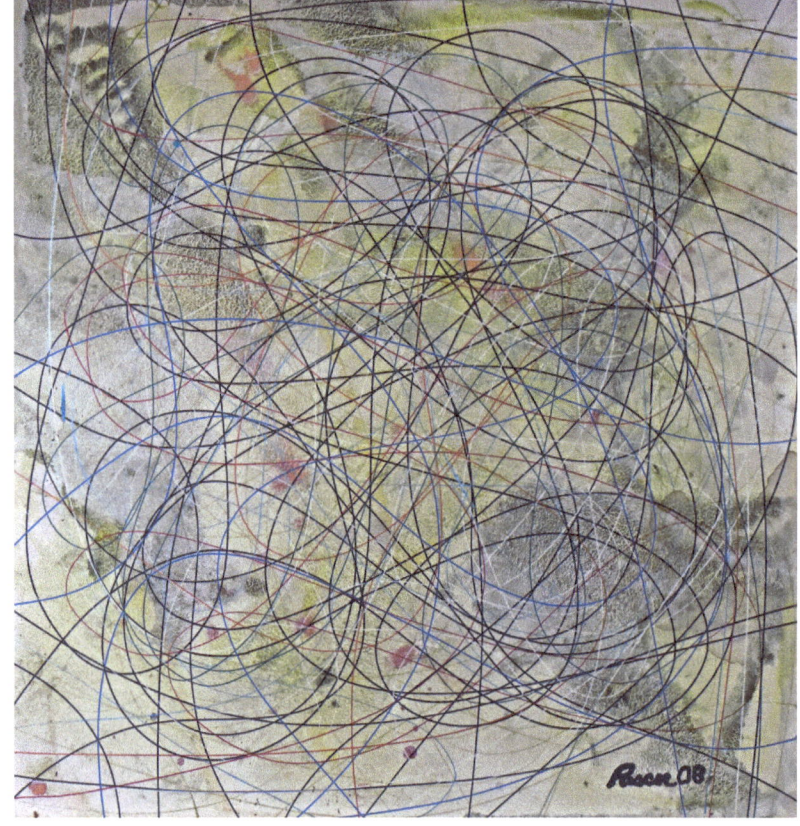

2009

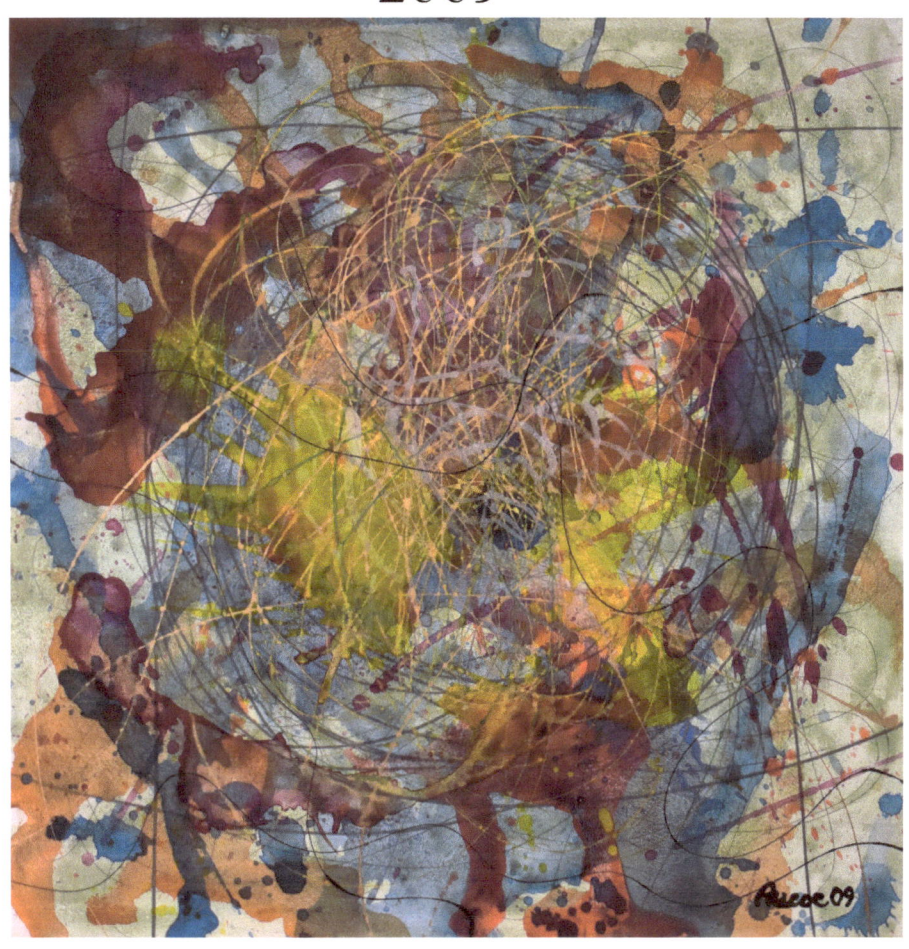

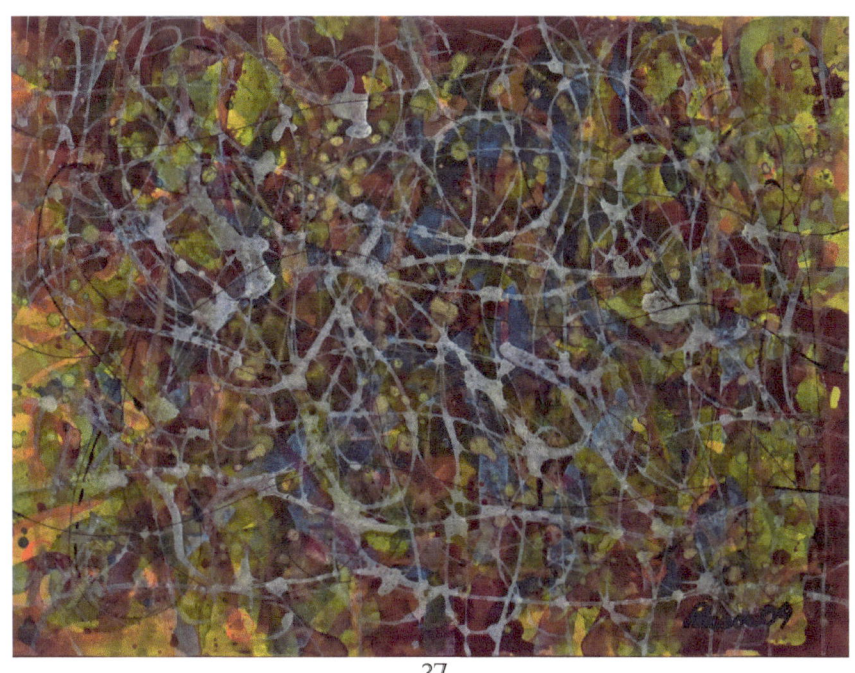

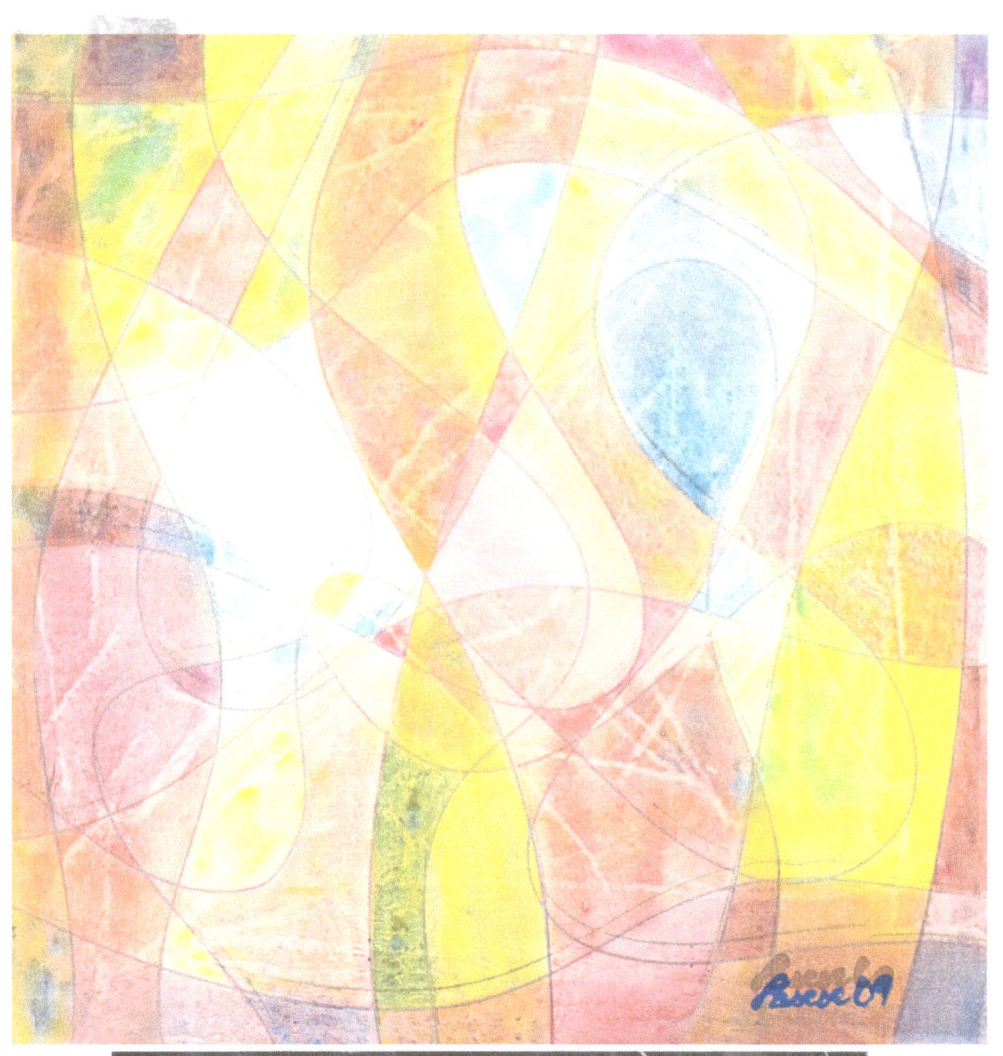
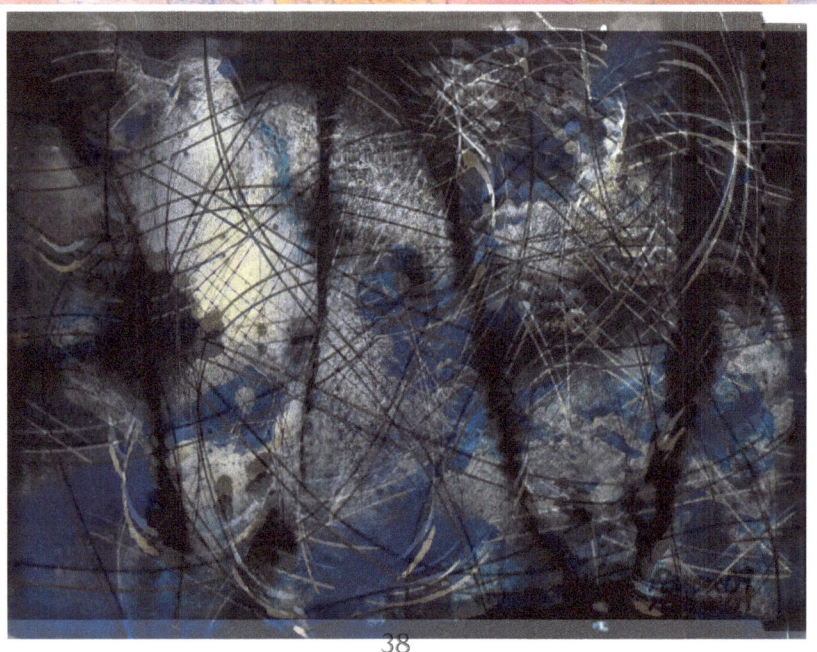

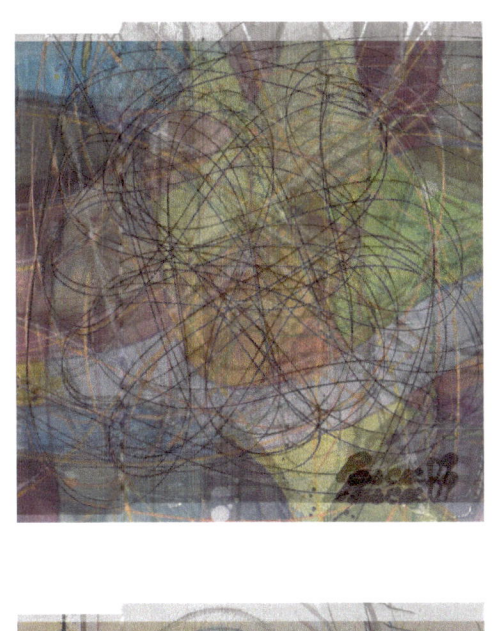
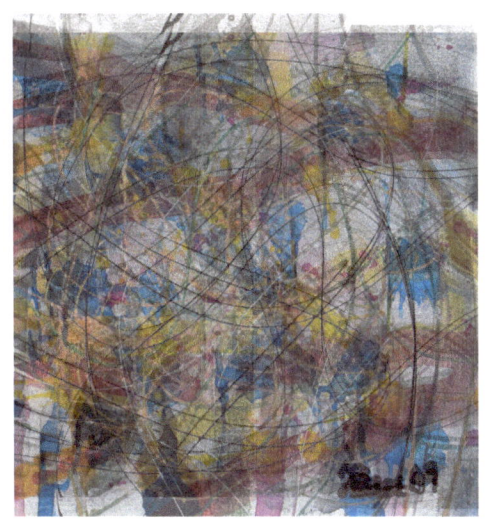
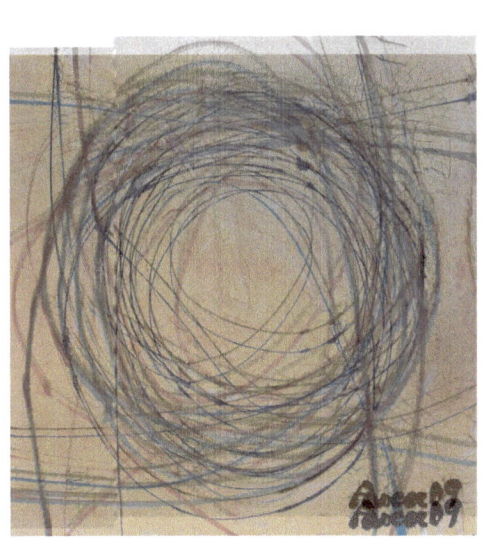
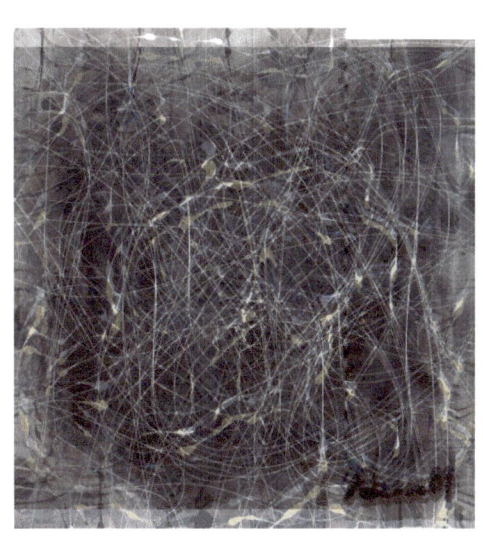
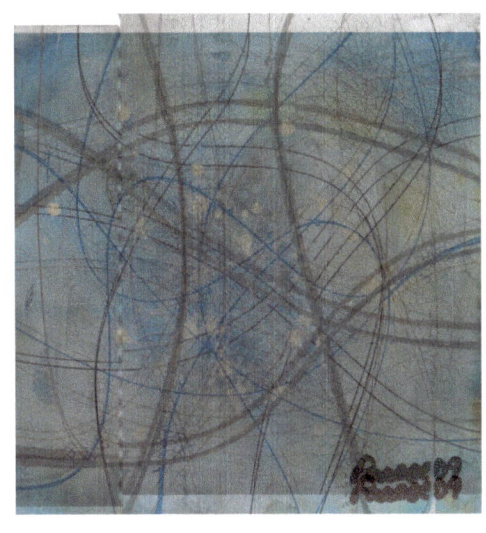
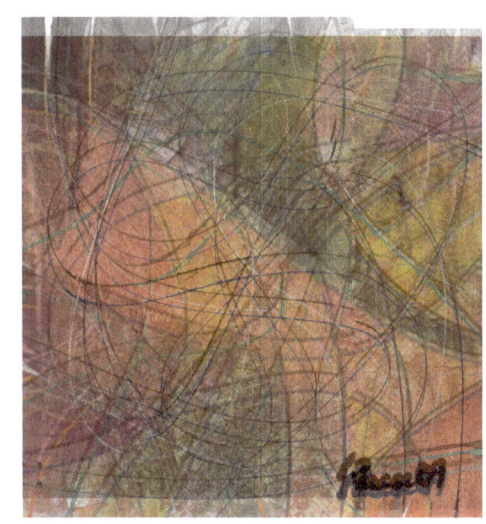

2010

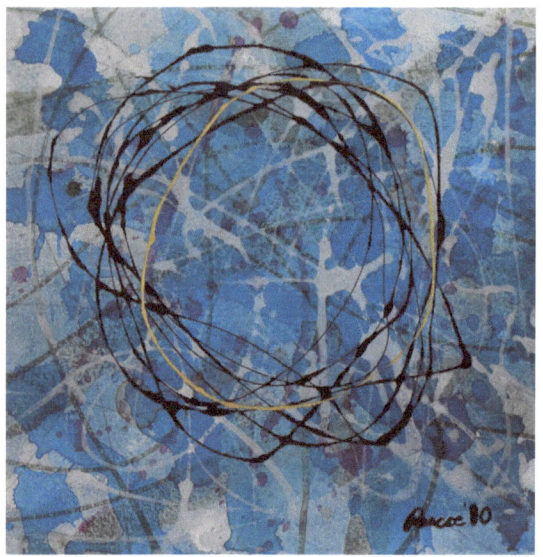

2011

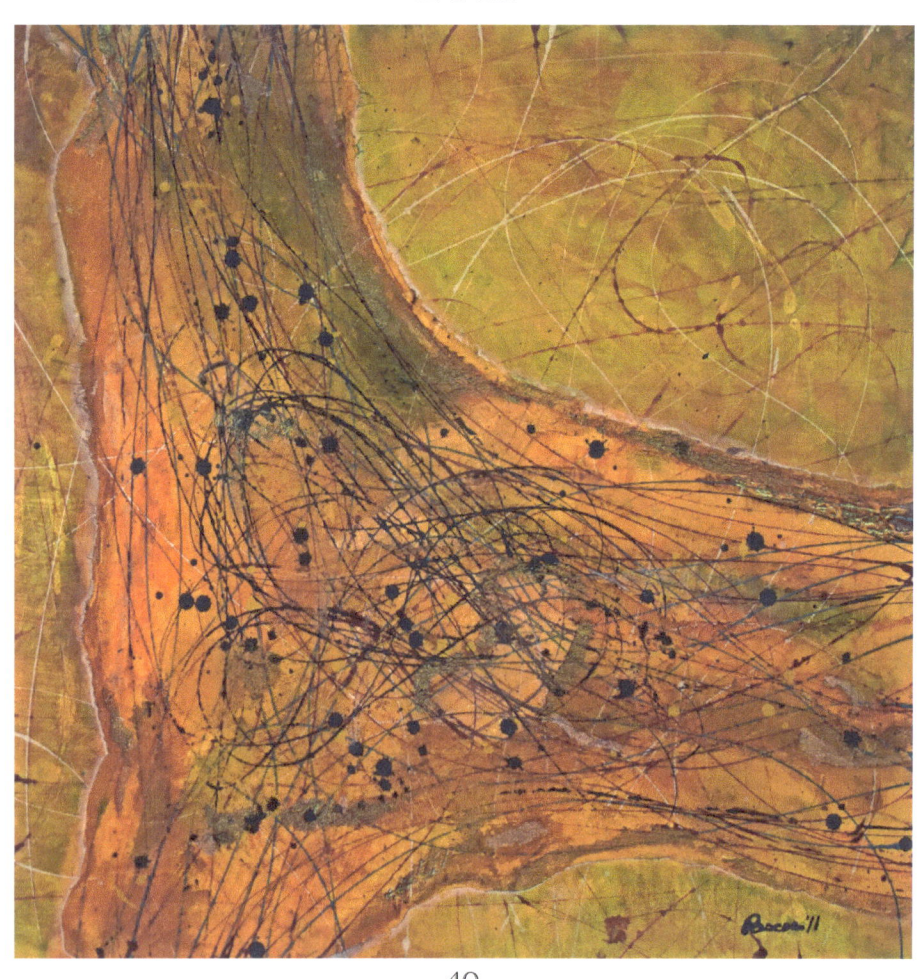

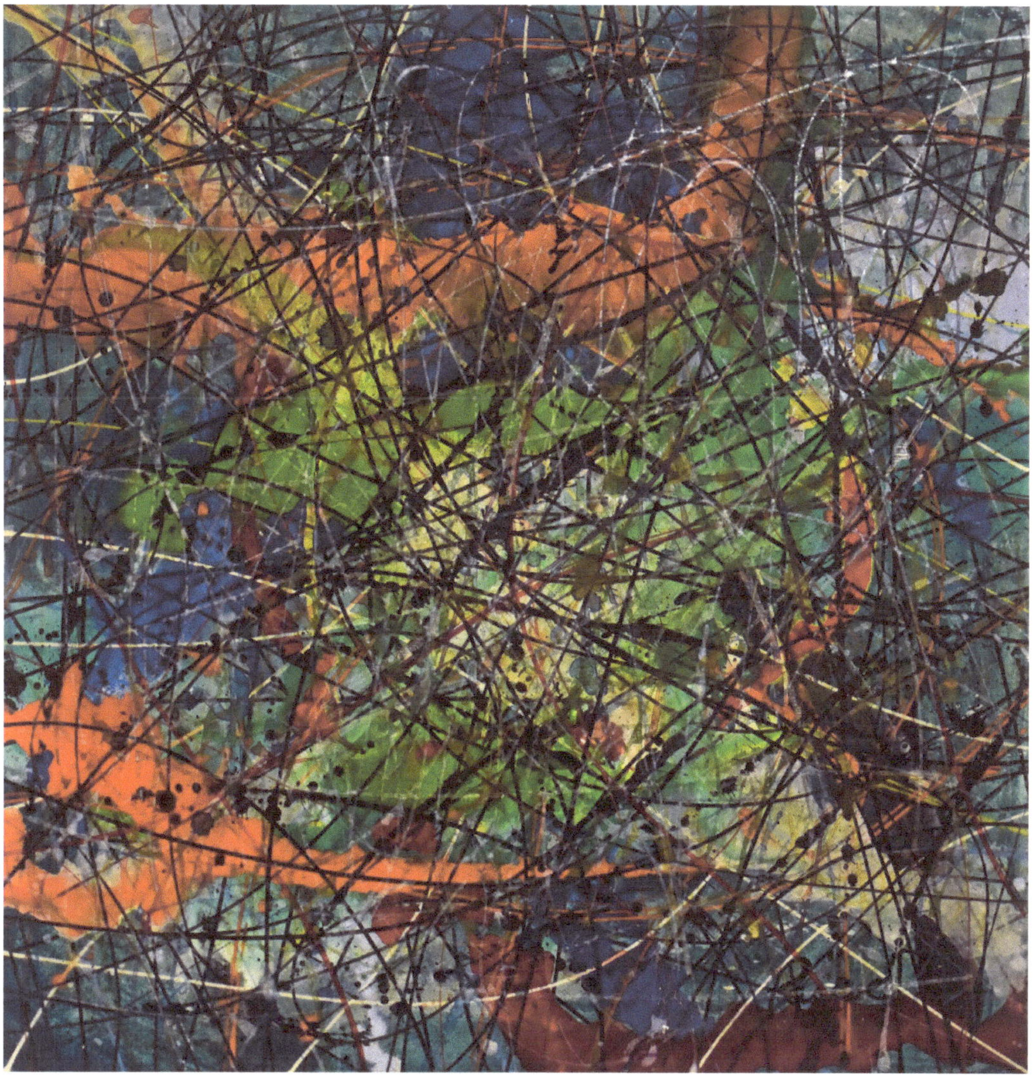

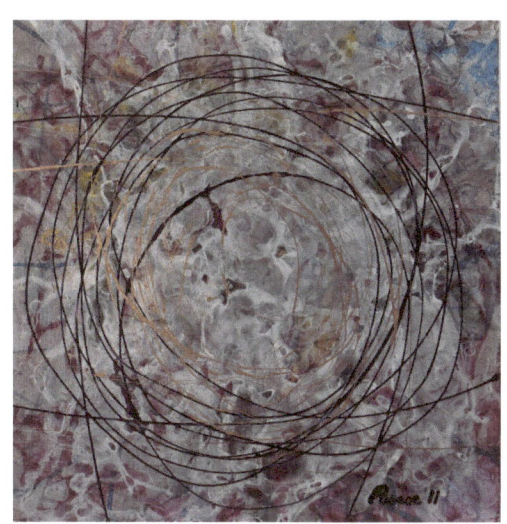
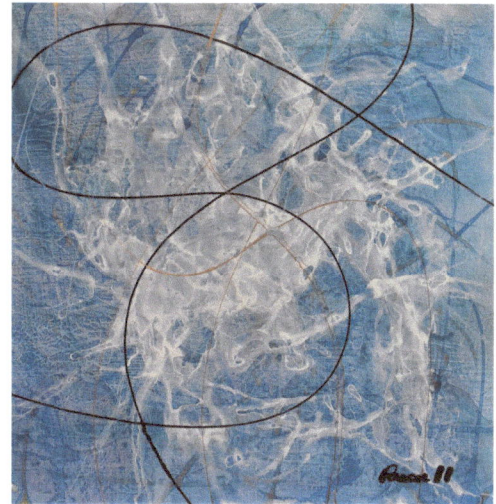

2013

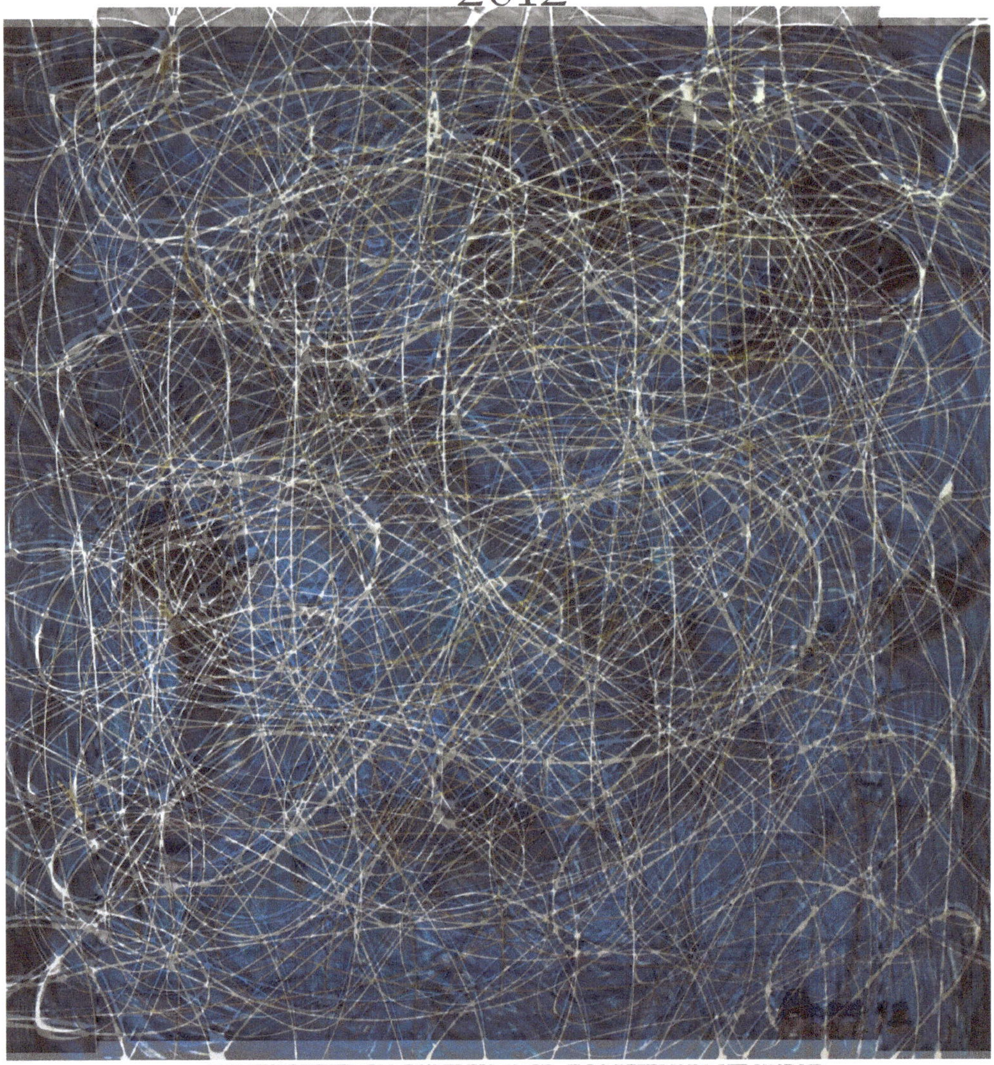

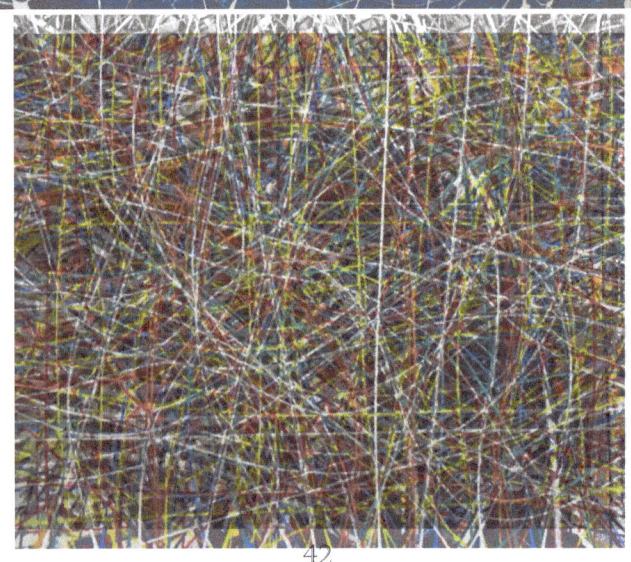

42

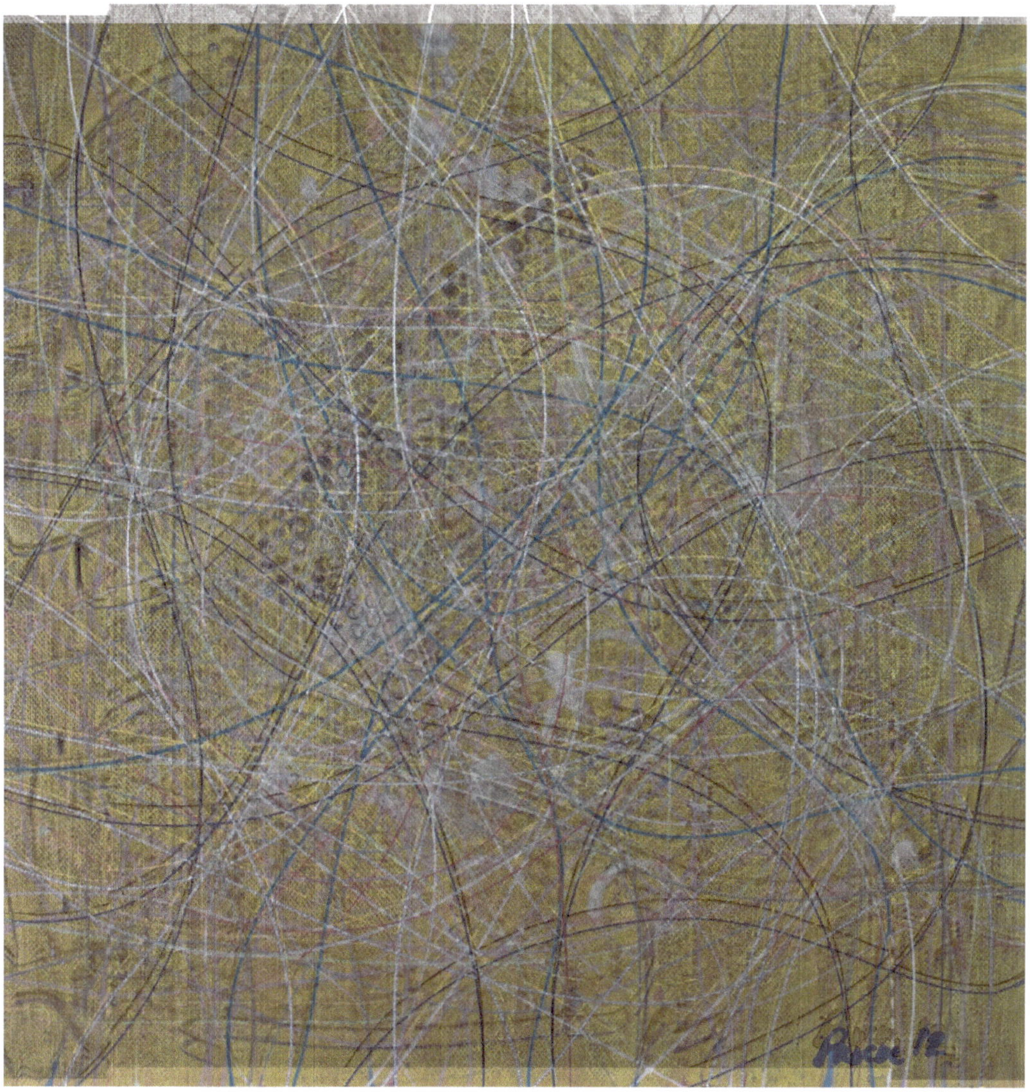

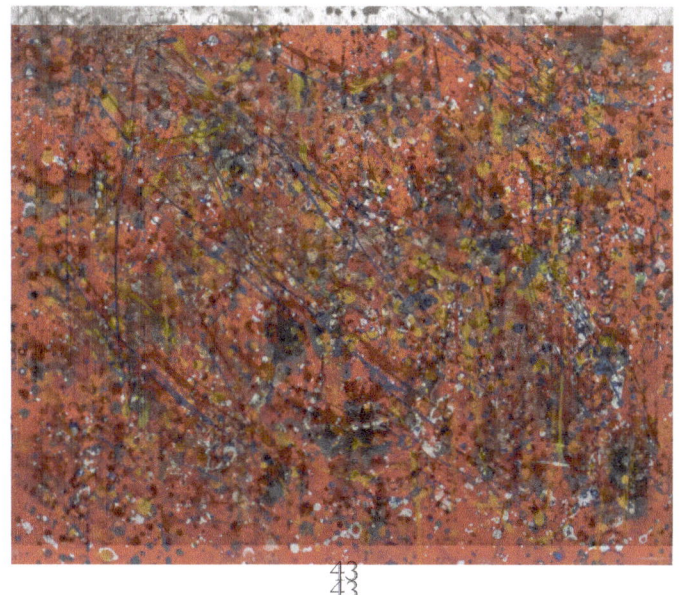

Undated Late

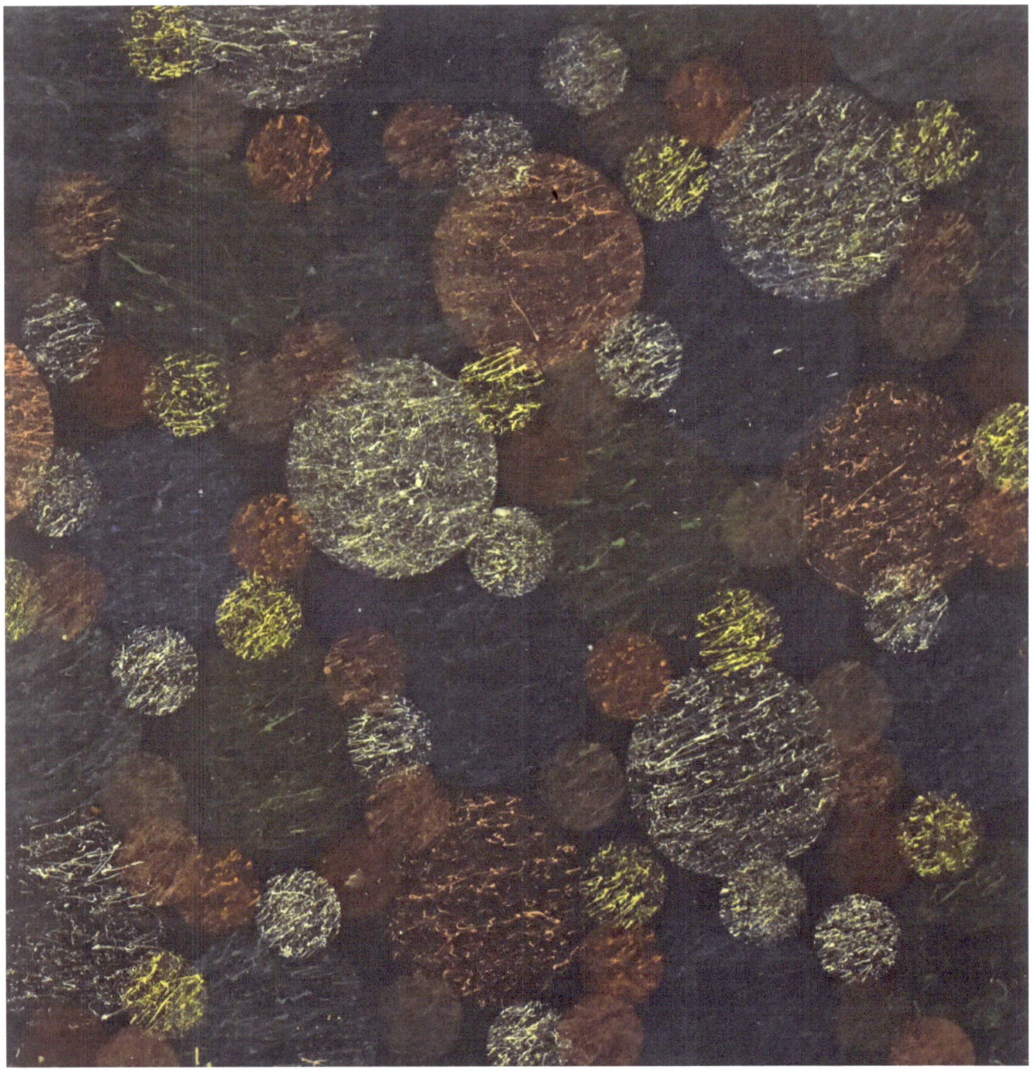

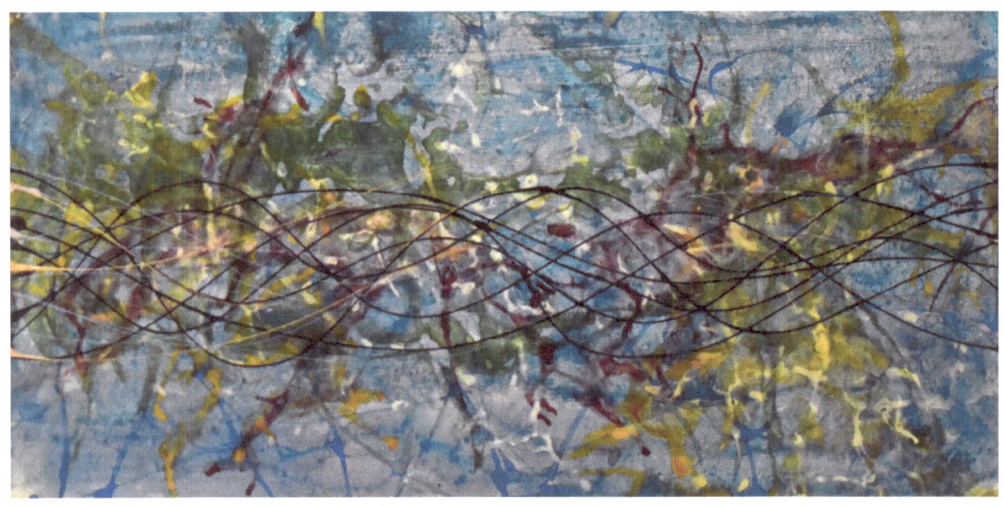

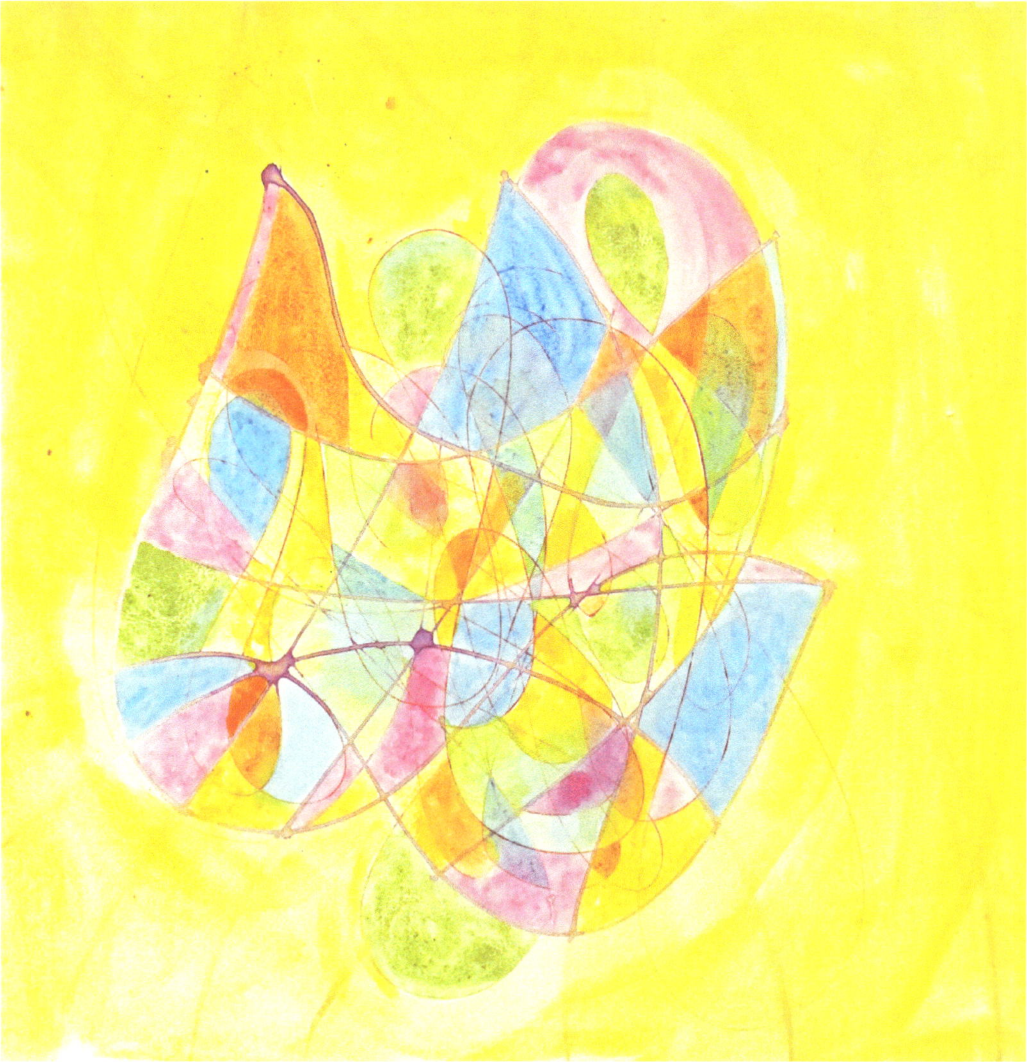

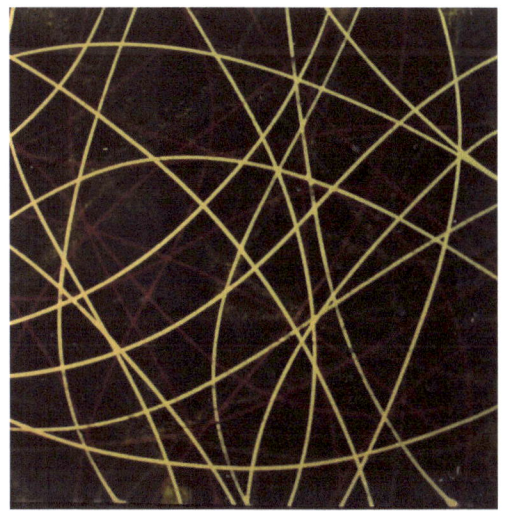
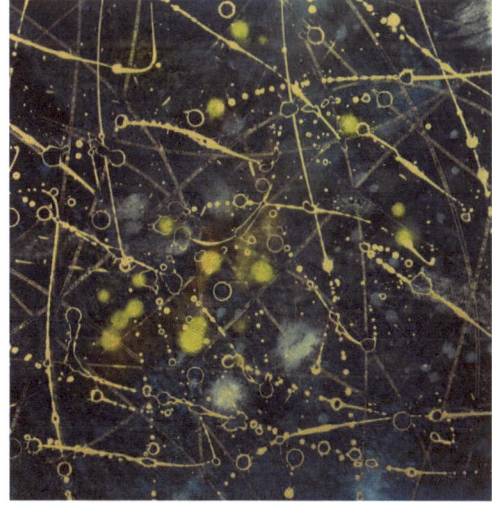

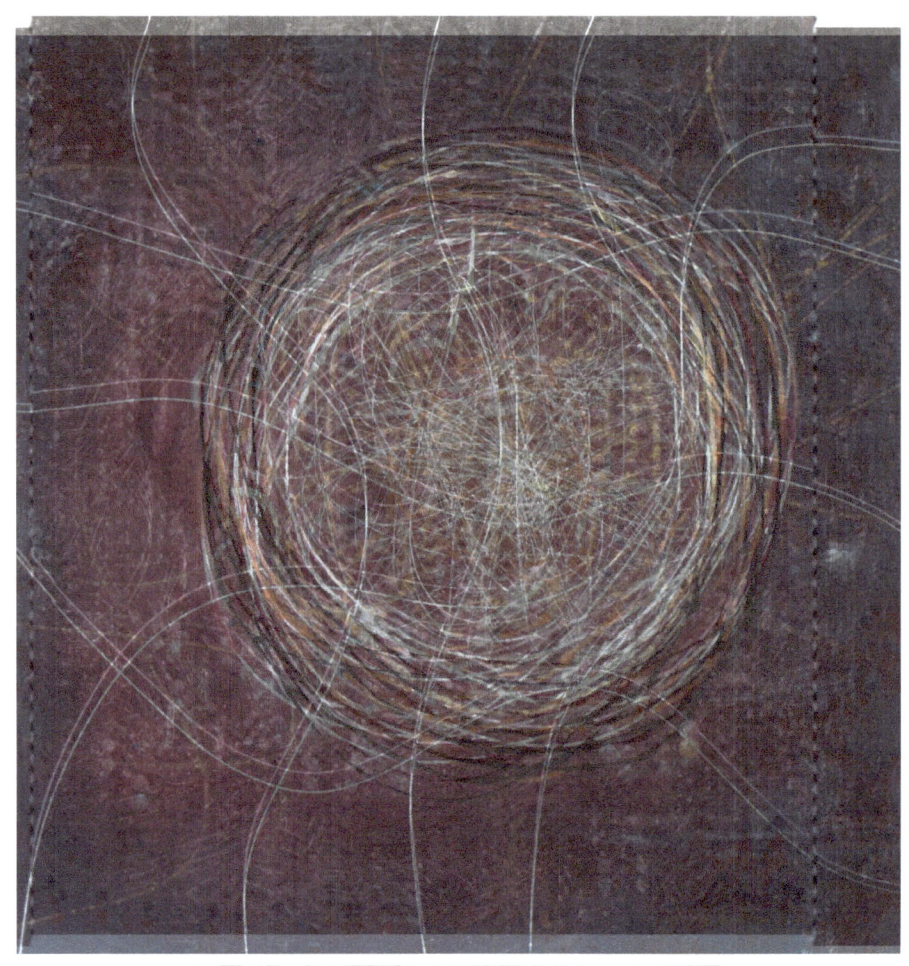
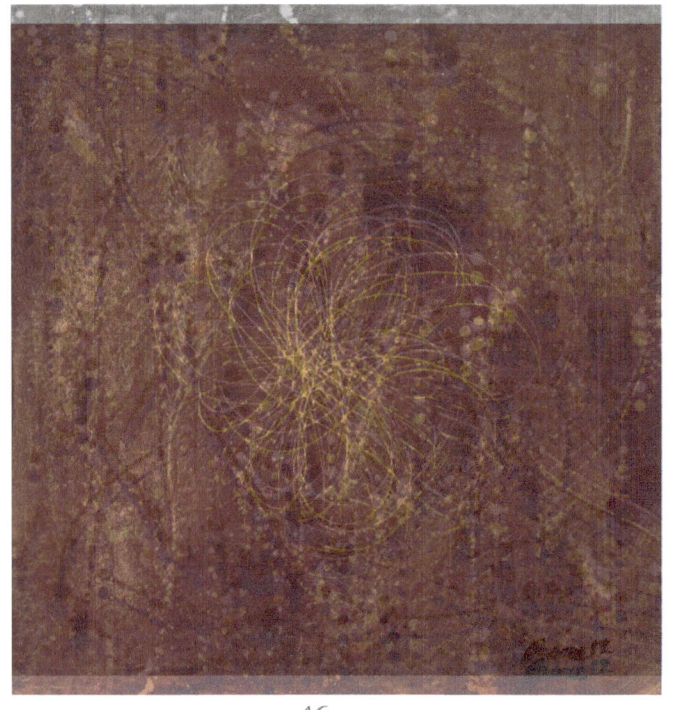

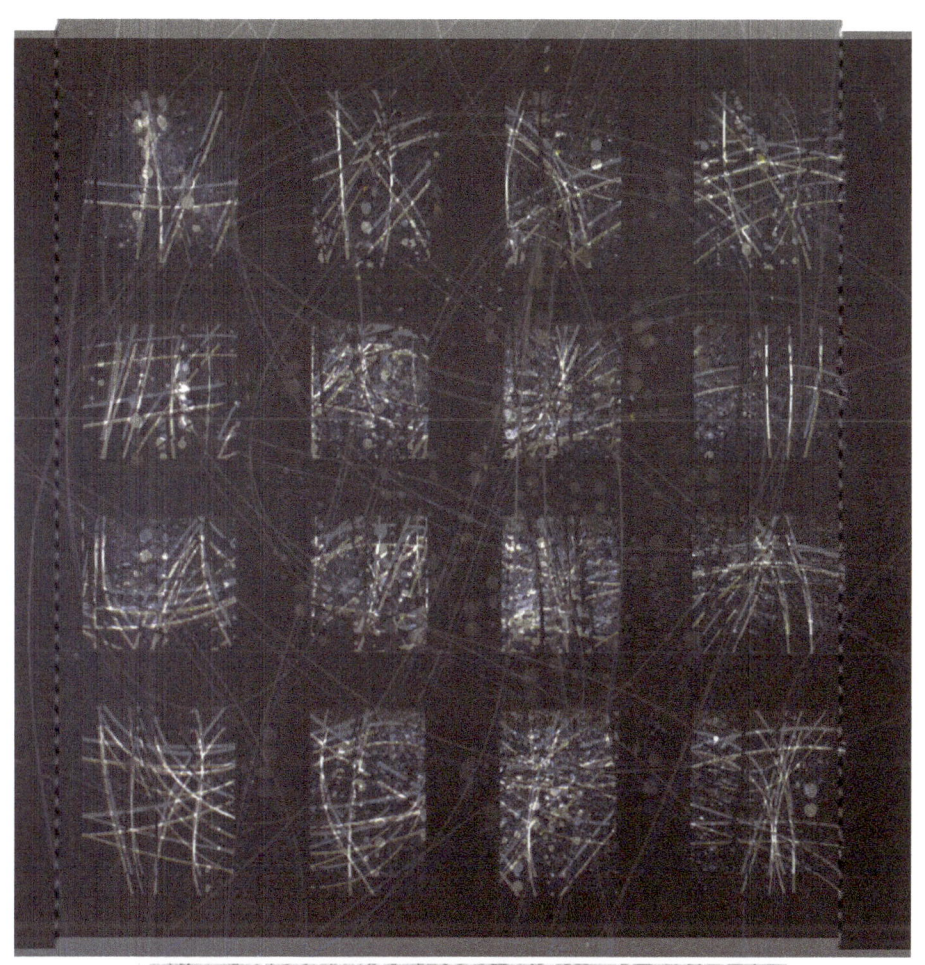
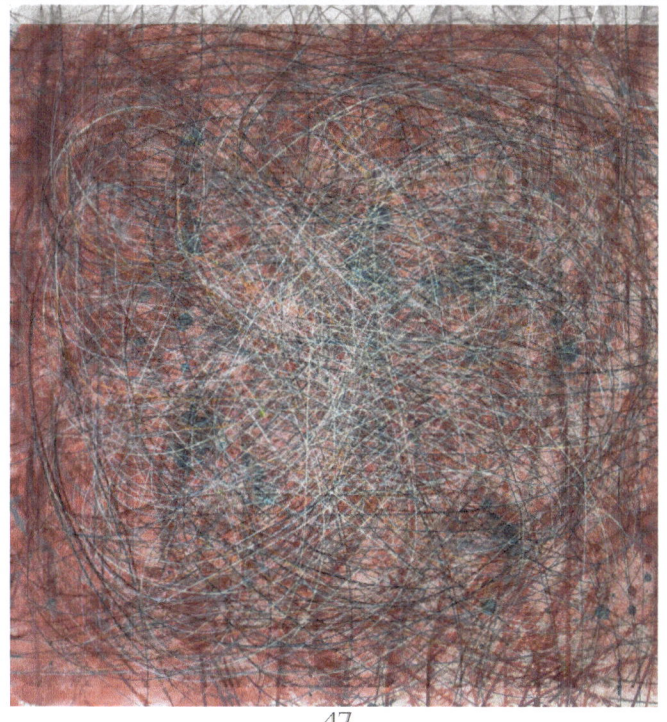

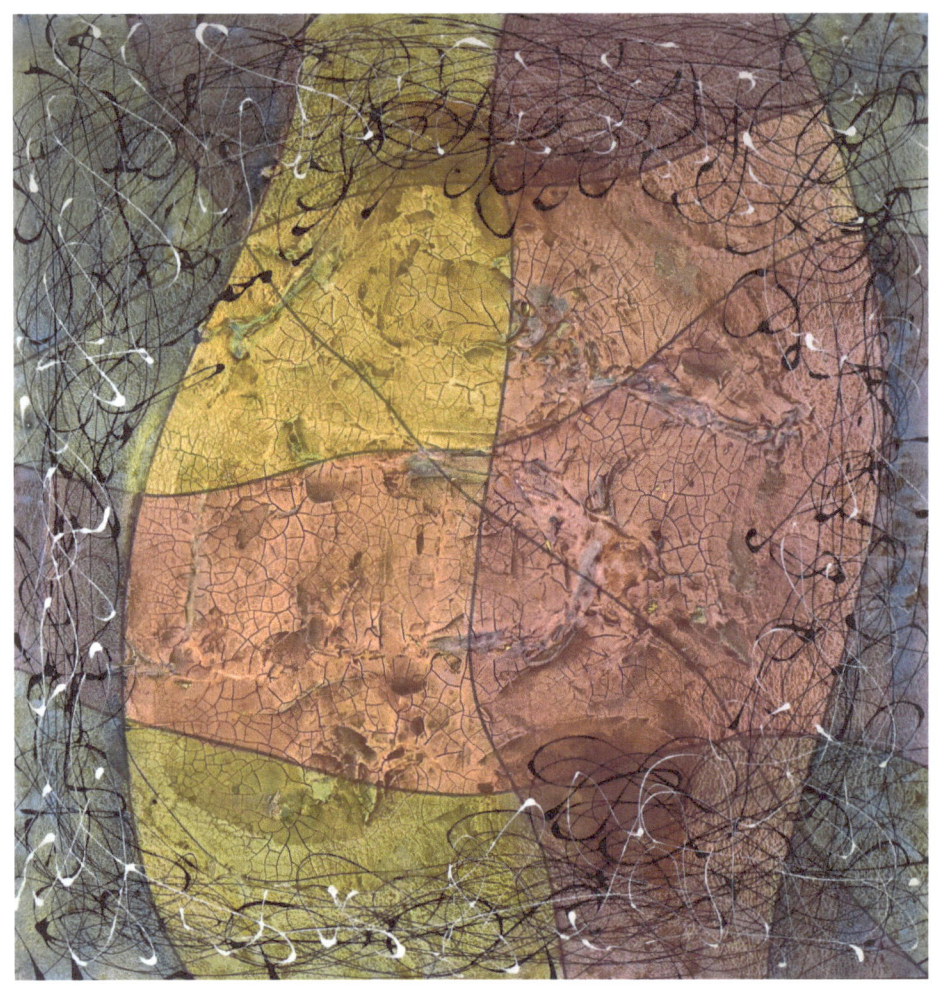
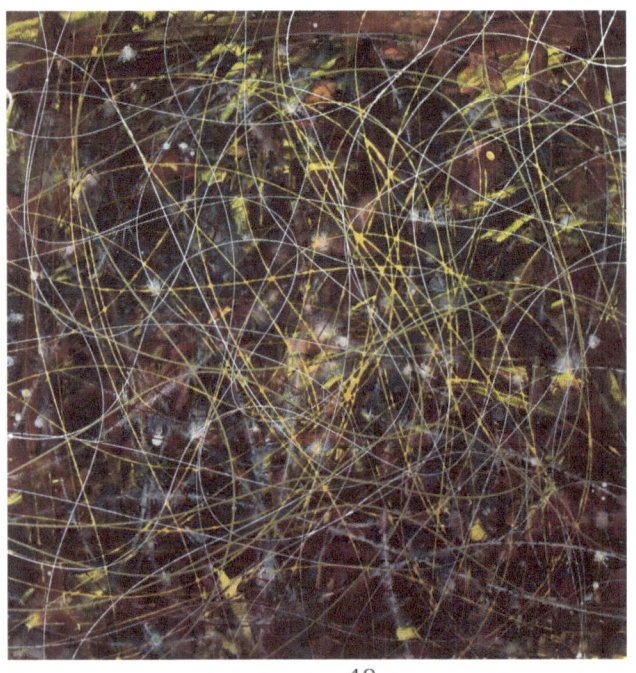

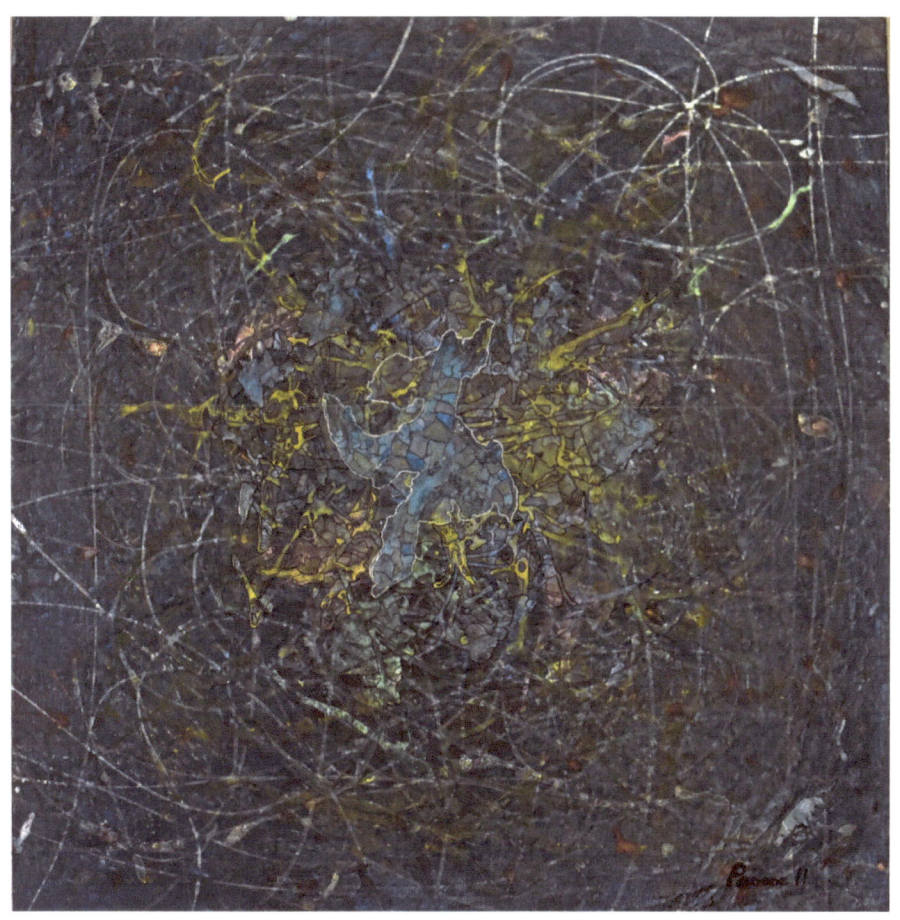

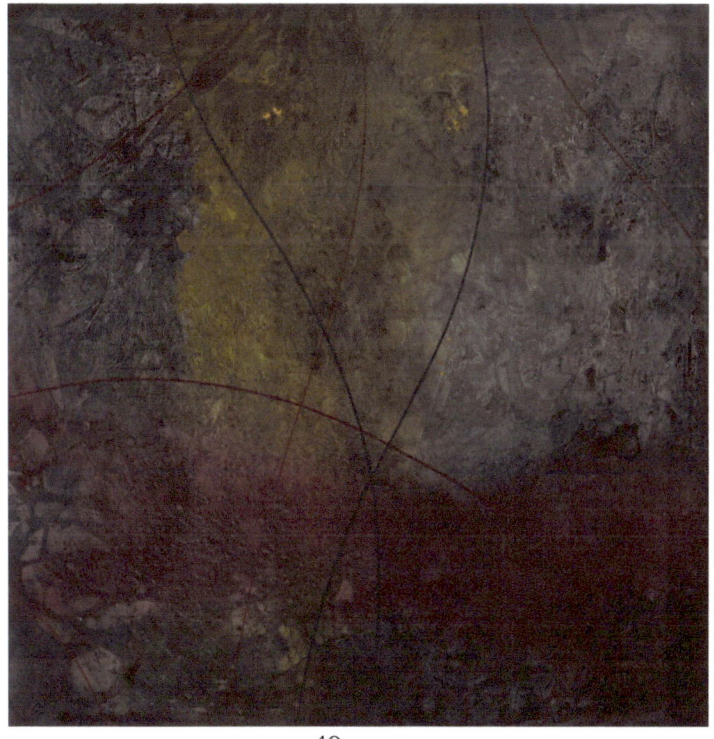

www.ingramcontent.com/pod-product-compliance
Lightning Source LLC
Chambersburg PA
CBHW051927210526
45473CB00006B/2159